Home is the Halifax

Home is the Halifax

An extraordinary account of rebuilding
a classic WWII bomber and creating the
Yorkshire Air Museum to house it

Ian Robinson MBE

decd. October 2010

Grub Street • London

Published by
Grub Street
4 Rainham Close
London
SW11 6SS

British Library Cataloguing in Publication Data
Robinson, Ian, 1925-
Home is the Halifax: an extraordinary account of
rebuilding a classic WWII bomber and creating the
Yorkshire Air Museum to house it.
1. Halifax (Bomber) – Conservation and restoration.
2. Yorkshire Air Museum – History.
I. Title
623.7'463'0288-dc22

ISBN-13: 9781906502775

Cover design by Sarah Driver

Book design by Roy Platten, Eclipse, Hemel Hempstead.
roy.eclipse@btopenworld.com

Printed and bound in Slovenia by DZS Graphic.

Grub Street Publishing only uses
FSC (Forest Stewardship Council) paper for its books.

The publisher would especially like to thank *FlyPast* magazine for permission
to use the images between pages 73/74 and 83/84.

Contents

Foreword

This book is about dogged determination, arising from convinced Yorkshire logic. And lest you think these words are too fawning, they come from a Lancastrian!

Ian Robinson's background gave him the sense of heritage, and his personality provided all the attributes necessary to see an ambitious project through to its glorious achievement.

The thinking was straightforward. There should be a Halifax on show at Elvington, where once Handley Page's under-praised stalwart flew on 'ops'. There was no chance of an original, so the job was to *recreate* one, using as many genuine, or kindred, components as possible. A hen coop that once bashed the circuit at Stornoway, a Berlin Airlift-era Hastings, engines from a French transport, contributions from friends and colleagues worldwide, all contributed to the formation of a masterpiece – Friday the 13th.

Cries of "It's not a *proper* one!" didn't faze Ian and his team. But the detractors couldn't see how moved former air and ground crew were at being reunited with *their* warhorse.

I could have no better proof than when I phoned Ian to ask a favour. Could I bring a friend to see Friday? He had trained as a mid-upper gunner on Halifaxes and it would make an emotive birthday present. Typically, the answer was an unhesitating 'yes'. Derek got to revisit his 'office' and spent a while deep in reflection. Since its inception, Friday has always been a 'people's aircraft' – Ian and the Yorkshire Air Museum would have it no other way.

Today's increasingly bureaucratic and beige-coloured world could do with more people of Ian Robinson's ilk.

Ken Ellis
Editor *FlyPast*

Introduction and Acknowledgements

When I came home after a spell in hospital in November 2008, my dear wife frequently told me that recording my experiences at the Yorkshire Air Museum Allied Air Forces Memorial from 1983 to 1999 would be therapeutic. Several friends joined in, and eventually I gave in and started writing what is now *Home is the Halifax*. How right they were. I'm sure there are lots of incidents which I've forgotten about, but memories – happy memories – came flooding back.

In the early 1980s whenever the thought of retirement entered my head, my main concern was how I'd fill my spare time. Having always been fully employed since the age of sixteen, the prospect of too much time on my hands was a bit frightening. But I needn't have worried.

In 1983 I read an article in *The Yorkshire Post* which included an emotive photo of a flight of Jet Provosts over-flying Elvington airfield. Stood watching were Rachel Semlyen and Squadron Leader Ian Wormald. The article went on to explain they were considering establishing a museum on the site of the World War Two bomber base at Elvington in North Yorkshire. I was thrilled at the prospect having had a long-standing association with flying in Yorkshire, which thanks to them has now continued to this very day. We joined forces and soon people of all ages and from all corners of the country were keen to follow.

In those early days Rachel and I attended many squadron reunions which were taking place in various parts of the country to drum up support. One I vividly remember was in Harrogate when 433 Squadron, Royal Canadian Air Force had gathered and we met many veterans who had flown Halifaxes from Skipton-on-Swale. One individual who became a great friend had served as a squadron leader pilot, and he was full of enthusiasm for the project. His name was Wib Pierce and he was typical of literally hundreds of Canadians whom we came to know, including General Reg Lane and General J. Hull. At all of these reunions we met with so much encouragement and many people became donors, volunteers, friends, or all of those things! The Canadians were later to play a very significant part in the development of the museum and many happy occasions are referred to in this book.

Another name which springs to mind is Doug Dent. He served with 10 Squadron at Melbourne (Yorks) and during the post-war years he became a leading light in 10 Squadron Association. This squadron was in existence until fairly recently, flying VC10s, and Doug arranged flights for some of us when the squadron were carrying out air-to-air refuelling exercises. Colin Long also played such an important role in our development. He served with 35 Squadron who were the first to be equipped with the Halifax and he eventually became part of the pathfinder group. Both Doug and Colin loved the Halifaxes they worked on and woe betide any Lancaster man who got involved in the conversation.

I still have a copy of a document prepared for us by Chris Dunham. It records over 1,000 names and addresses of Yorkshire Air Museum members and is dated May 1989. Of course, some people were to leave us but many more were to join. In the beginning at Elvington visitors appeared from everywhere and many of them made generous offers to help us in our uphill struggle, as we had no financial resources at all.

Two such supporters were members of the guild of aviation artists (GAvA), Frank Wooton and John Rayson, both with a particular love of the Halifax. I had known John in the 1940s and some of his many contributions to the museum are recorded herewith. I wish I could recall the names of all those people who did join us, but writing this book has brought many faces in to my mind's eye, such a happy bunch of volunteers and good friends, many of whom are no longer with us. But every bit of help, no matter what form it took and no matter whether it is recorded here or not, was so much appreciated by me and by the trustees at the time.

Many ex-YAM volunteers meet at Sherburn Aero Club at Sherburn-in-Elmet, a Yorkshire airfield which was opened in the 1930s and used extensively during World War Two. It is now one of the UK's major flying clubs and frequently hosts prestigious events such as aerobatic championships and the like. The idea for this association of veterans and aviation enthusiasts came from the-then chairman of the club, Mr. Neville Binks and another ex-RAF flier, Mr. Don Hewett. Having formed the group, they were stumped for a name, although they wanted to incorporate the word 'bomber'. One day when the chief flying instructor, a well-known ex-RAF squadron leader, 'Jacko' Jackson crossed the car park into the clubhouse and remarked that with all these posh cars outside they were more like barons than bombers, the name stuck. And so the association known as Bomber Barons was formed. What happy meetings we have every Thursday, with a lot of banter, some reminiscing and a great deal of friendship. Membership is now well over 100 and one of the highlights of the year is the annual Christmas lunch, happily and competently organised by Nev and his wife Val.

Now to some heartfelt thanks. Most of the photographs in this book are from my personal collection. Others have been reproduced by kind permission from Roy Barnett, Ken Ellis of *FlyPast* magazine, John and Betty Hunt, Guy Jefferson, Dennis Sawden, Peter Slee, Mike Usherwood and Ian Wormald. In one or two instances I have been unable to trace the original owners and cannot therefore offer any acknowledgement.

My thanks to so many people who have helped in the preparation of this book. First, thanks to my dear wife Mary for all her hard work and tolerance. To Ken Ellis and Dennis Sawden for their constructive suggestions and encouragement, and also to Ian Wormald, John Bell, Tom James, Peter Slee, Norman Spence, Mike Usherwood and Guy Jefferson. Thanks to David Westwood, for his technical tuition on our steam-driven word processor and to John Davies and Sophie Campbell of Grub Street Publishing for their courtesy and endless patience.

My involvement with the Yorkshire Air Museum during those sixteen years from 1983 to 1999 gave me a lot of pleasure and a lot of satisfaction, not least because of all the interesting people I met. But most of all I'm proud to think that I made a contribution, with a lot of help and a lot of luck, to what is a fitting memorial to all those who gave their lives in Bomber Command during World War Two.

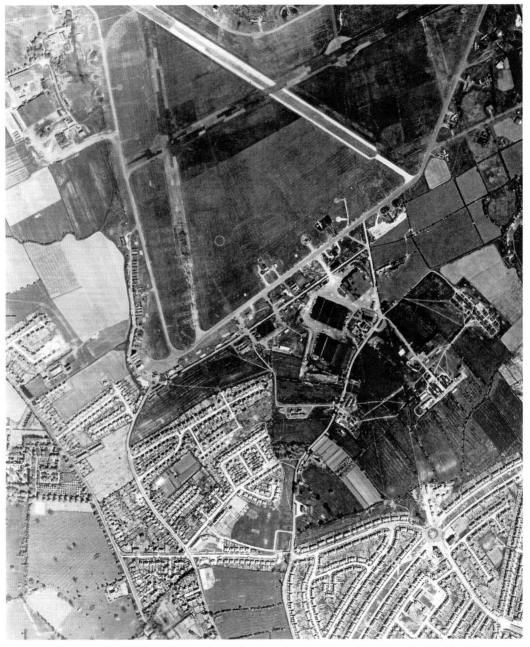

Aerial photo of Clifton airfield where the author was based during the war, taken in 1946. Now a huge trading estate with hundreds of houses. (English Heritage [NMR] RAF Photography)

This is to certify that (insert full name in capitals)
Mr.
Mrs. ROBINSON ...
Miss
holder of National Registration Card KSMI/15
whose photograph and description is contained herein
is a ... British ... subject and is employed by the
AIR MINISTRY or the MINISTRY OF AIRCRAFT PRODUCTION

STATION OR ESTABLISHMENT AT WHICH EMPLOYED

Date	Station	Signature and rank of officer certifying

Description
Height 6' 1"   Build Slim
Colour of eyes brown   Colour of hair brown
Date and place of birth 4.8.1925
Cross Hills, Keighley

Signature of holder ... J. Robin
Signature of ...

FORM 2185

ROYAL AIR FORCE

IDENTITY CARD FOR CIVILIANS
EMPLOYED BY THE AIR MINISTRY
OR THE MINISTRY OF AIRCRAFT
PRODUCTION AT ROYAL AIR FORCE
STATIONS AND ESTABLISHMENTS

No. 232157

Above: *Author's identity card.*

Right: *Author with father, mother and sister.*

CHAPTER 1 Wartime Flying in Yorkshire

60 MAINTENANCE UNIT

Having won a scholarship to Keighley Technical College in 1939, my studies for a BSc were interrupted by a certain Adolf Hitler, but my ambition had always been to join the Royal Air Force under a scheme whereby entry was available to the sons of Class E RAF Reservists. My father came into this category having served in the Royal Flying Corps during World War One. Because of this, he was called up a few months before the outbreak of the Second World War and posted to York to set up 60 RAF Maintenance Unit at a village just outside the city – Shipton-by-Beningbrough. With so many airfields being established throughout the UK these units were essential for the recovery and repair of crashed aeroplanes. In the case of Yorkshire, this task was undertaken by 60 MU. Several hundred personnel of all trades, with fleets of Coles cranes and Queen Mary articulated lorries became fully occupied visiting twenty-four or so airfields and a tragic amount of crash sites, to dismantle and remove the remains of some 3,000 incidents – many of course resulting in fatalities.

With so many involving military aeroplanes throughout the Vale of York, the sight of 50-foot-long Queen Marys was very common. When one bears in mind that aeroplanes and their crews could not always choose where to 'put down', damaged and crashed aeroplanes sometimes had to be collected from the most inaccessible places. Once an incident had been reported, a team would leave Shipton-by-Beningbrough with lifting equipment and the necessary means of transport, and as the work involved several different tradesmen, the first thing the flight sergeant in charge had to do was to fix-up overnight accommodation for all the crew. There were many amusing and complex situations and one in particular involved a Spitfire which had made a wheels-up landing close to the Parkway Hotel between Bramhope and Leeds. With the hotel being so convenient, Flight Sergeant Robinson asked the hotel manager for accommodation for the whole of the team. The manager readily agreed. After two nights' stay and with the Spitfire dismantled and loaded, he asked the hotel manager to fill in the requisite forms to claim payment for the accommodation. Surprise, surprise, on the back of the form was a list of the rates the RAF was prepared to pay. They were considerably less than the manager was expecting. His face fell when he saw that he could only claim something like two shillings per person per night.

Top: *Officers and NCOs, 60 MU, July 1945.* Above: *All ranks of 60 MU.*

Bearing in mind that most of the squadrons in Yorkshire were equipped with Halifaxes (see page 17), a total of 461 accidents is not a surprising figure. 147 Wellingtons and 100 Whitleys made up the next largest losses. It is important to note that these figures do not include aeroplanes which did not return from operations. The total number of losses in Bomber Command was 55,000 personnel. Not all crashes involved loss of life but many did. At the Stonefall cemetery in Forest Lane, Harrogate, there are over 1,000 graves of air force personnel, of which 60% served with the Royal Canadian Air Force. Others are from the dominions and the Royal Air Force. A walk amongst the headstones indicates that the average age of death would be about twenty.

Queen Mary low loader, 60 MU.

The cemetery is managed by the Commonwealth War Graves Commission and it is beautifully maintained. Some sixty-five years after the end of World War Two, people in the county of Yorkshire continue to erect memorials to the many thousands who lost their lives and readers will understand why the memorial aspect of the Yorkshire Air Museum is vitally important to so many people.

When the Yorkshire-based bomber aircraft were returning to their bases, it was not uncommon through errors in navigation at night to overshoot the Vale of York and unintentionally fly into the Pennines, often with fatal results. Thus, 60 MU would set forth into the Dales to collect what remained of downed aircraft, and as many readers will know there were several hump-backed bridges en route. Frequently, one of the Queen Marys (which were very long and low-slung) grounded on these bridges. On the positive side, many of the Dales villagers were excited to see 'the military' arrive in their small hamlets. One village which seemed to figure more than once was Kettlewell, and of course the teams had to be billeted somewhere

Stonefall cemetery, Harrogate.

He 111 shot down on Yorkshire's east coast. Picked up by 60 MU, 1940.

nearby, where the hospitality of the villagers knew no bounds and many lifelong friendships were established.

Needless to say, the RAF ground facilities had not kept pace with the advances in the aeroplanes. One amusing incident occurred involving a German Heinkel He 111 and the then Flt Lt Peter Townsend (later to become group captain and well-known because of his romance with Princess Margaret). The aeroplane had been shot at south of Whitby and Townsend claimed 1/3 of this 'kill'. This was the first German aircraft to crash on English soil. Flight Sergeant Robinson and his team were despatched to dismantle and recover this, their first enemy aeroplane. The engine fitters, working to a set procedure, attempted to remove the engines. "Hey, chiefy, the spanners don't fit" – of course not, the nuts were metric!

Ju 88 August 1940, 60 MU.

Flight Sergeant Robinson (the author's father) and team at the crash site, Gt. Whernside.

Me 109 being assembled by 60 MU in York to raise money for Spitfire week, 1940.

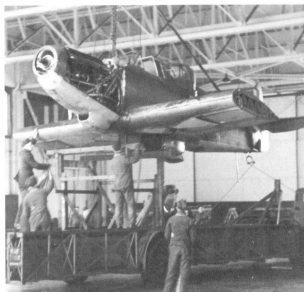

Boulton and Paul Defiant, October 1940, being worked on by 60 MU.

Because of the often inaccessible crash sites, the local army and police were frequently called upon to guard the aeroplanes, and one almost-unique incident occurred on a hill-top near Pateley Bridge in August 1944. One Halifax from a conversion unit whilst on a night flight, belly-landed on the very top of a hill, about 1,200 feet above sea level. The only injury sustained was to the pilot who got a crack on the head when the aeroplane de-celerated from about 180 mph to zero in something like 70 yards. The 60 MU team, with no vehicular access, then had to dismantle and transport the bits of the aeroplane in manageable sections (in total about 25 tons) down the hillside.

One memorable evening, my father and I, with a young lady who should perhaps remain nameless, were driving from Aldwark Bridge – a small village about twelve miles from York – heading for The Green Tree, a pub in the nearby village of Little Ouseburn, when a Whitley from RAF Linton-on-Ouse carried out a most graceful belly-landing in front of our very eyes. Needless to say, we never did get to the pub.

Mk V Whitley after a wheels-up landing.

Enjoying a pint at the famous wartime pub near Nun Monkton, Linton-on-Ouse.

The recovery of aeroplanes could be a hazardous undertaking as sometimes they crashed with the undercarriage retracted, and at that time lifting gear had not been designed to cope with 30-ton aeroplanes, sometimes on very soft ground. Another Halifax from Linton-on-Ouse had in fact belly-landed with wheels up, and after the jacks had been placed in position, the aeroplane slithered sideways and killed an armourer who was just about to de-fuse the bomb load.

It may interest readers to know that a highly respected aviation historian, Guy Jefferson, BEM, researched crash sites in the county of Yorkshire involving military aircraft only and which occurred between 1930 and 1980. Obviously the majority of these incidents took place in World War Two 1939-1945. Nevertheless, the total during the fifty years mentioned was 1,803 of which 85% were wartime crashes as listed by type, as follows.

Aircraft	No.	Aircraft	No.	Aircraft	No.
Halifax (all Mks)	461	Stirling	7	Neptune	2
Whitley (all Mks)	100	B.A. Lightning	6	Dakota	2
Mosquito (all Mks)	70	Venom	4	Hamilcar (glider)	1
Tiger Moth	33	Tomahawk	4	Valentia	1
Junkers 88 (all Mks)	16	Avro York	3	Mitchell	1
Hawker Audax	13	Gladiator	3	Canberra	1
Magister	10	Valetta	3	Hawker Henley	1
Chipmunk	8	Barracuda	2	Varsity	1
Hunter	7	Phantom	2		
H.P. Harrow	5	Hotspur (glider)	2	Spitfire (all Mks)	115
Beaufort	4	Proctor	1	Beaufighter	72
Typhoon	3	Buckmaster	1	Jet Provost (all Mks)	37
S.A. Bulldog	3	Aerocobra	1	Vampire (all Mks)	19
Liberator	3	Lockheed Electra	1	Miles Master	14
Piston Provost	2	Sea Prince	1	Sabre	11
Messerschmitt 210	2	Hadrian (glider)	1	Dornier 217	8
Hawker Hart	2			Heinkel 111	7
Manchester	1	Meteor (all Mks)	119	Fairey Battle	5
Albermarle	1	Lancaster (all Mks)	78	Hastings	4
Hawker Hector	1	Airspeed Oxford	45	Buccaneer	4
Gnat	1	Hurricane	30	Botha	4
Albacore	1	Lysander	14	Avro Tutor	3
Brigand	1	Hornet	11	Fairchild Argus	2
		Harvard	8	Lincoln	2
Wellington (all Mks)	147	Martinet	7	Javelin	2
Blenheim (all Mks)	81	Heyford	6	Hawker Hind	1
Hampden	58	Warwick	4	Avro Vulcan	1
Lockheed Hudson	29	Flying Fortress	4	Rapide	1
Avro Anson (all Mks)	16	Whirlwind (helicopter)	3	Flamingo	1
Mustang	12	Hawker Demon	3	Gauntlet	1
Defiant	10	Sycamore (helicopter)	3	Wapiti	1

The wartime system covering military crashes involved a visit from an RAF inspector, usually along with a representative from the manufacturing company. Crashes were categorised into A, AC, B, E, and E2. Category A usually indicated a repair by the RAF on site. AC involved a civilian repair team from the manufacturers. B entailed dismantling by the RAF and subsequent transporting to the manufacturer's repair depot. E indicated that the aeroplane was a write-off, but some parts could be salvaged and used on other similar aeroplanes. Finally, category E2 was where an aeroplane had burnt and nothing could be used again.

The most common cause of crashes in the case of Halifaxes involved 'belly-landings'. This was where a pilot had to land his aeroplane with the undercarriage still retracted for whatever reason, and such incidents were usually classified as category B. Accidents involving fatalities were sadly common, brought about frequently by engine failure on take-off. Whilst the Vale of York was ideal for the location of military airfields, it is bordered by the Pennines in the west and by The Wolds and Howardian hills to the north and east. Having carried out raids over Europe at night, damaged aeroplanes (often carrying wounded members of the crew) could easily lose their bearings and at a flying speed of over 200 mph, over-flying their bases would often result in tragically crashing into the hills.

To the best of my knowledge, well over 1,500 crashed aeroplanes were recovered; another Halifax in the Lake District at Great Carrs, having crashed and killed the crew, was never recovered.

Whilst staying in Aldwark, I was escorting a young lady on a Sunday afternoon walk on the edge of the airfield at Linton when three twin-engined aircraft in formation at fairly low altitude were flying towards us. "What type are those?" asked my companion. "Oh, don't worry, those are Blenheims." As I spoke the last word, the bombs went off – and those 'Blenheims' were in fact Junkers Ju 88s. I quickly learned quite a bit about aircraft recognition.

MY INVOLVEMENT WITH AVIATION

How and why did I become involved with the Yorkshire Air Museum and the Halifax story? As I mentioned earlier, it was always my ambition to join the RAF, but sadly with the outbreak of war the procedure for the sons of Class E Reservists to be given priority was abandoned. And so I had to get a job.

The winding down team of the Handley Page, YARD at the Water Lane site, early 1948.

Aircrew trainees inspecting Mk V Halifax, 1943.

At about this time, Handley Page Ltd (manufacturers of the Halifax) had sent Eric Wardle Pickston to Clifton airfield, near York, to establish what was to become the York Aircraft Repair Depot (conveniently abbreviated to YARD). This would be about mid-to-late 1941. The depot was intended to repair – at the base or on site – the crashed Halifaxes based at the twenty-four airfields in Yorkshire. Perhaps I should mention here that in more than one book I've read recently, this establishment has been referred to as 48 Maintenance Unit. It was never a maintenance unit. It was from the very beginning the YARD – and to quote the jargon of the day, Handley Page Ltd were, 'managing agents for and on behalf of the Ministry of Aircraft Production'. (48 MU was located at Hawarden, near Chester, and was mainly concerned with Wellingtons.)

In the village of Rawcliffe nearby, some five T2 hangars were erected, and on the south-east side of the airfield a further eight T2s were built, known as the Water Lane site. These were still in existence up to 2009.

There was obviously a very close relationship between 60 MU at Shipton-by-Beningbrough and the YARD. And there were three categories of aeroplane at the latter:-

1. Complete overhaul and repair, usually taking about eight weeks to complete.
2. Aeroplane repair on operational airfields – a very variable timescale. The men sent out to do these repairs were known as 'outworkers' and usually travelled from the depot daily, but often had to be billeted near the stations involved.
3. Reduction of badly damaged aeroplanes in order to 'retrieve' spares.

The vast majority of 60 MU's work was understandably, collecting broken pieces of Halifaxes, and the main airframes retrieved were delivered to the YARD. Thus a binding link between the two was established and (no doubt over a pint) my father discussed my situation (as fathers do) with Eric Pickston, who told him that they were looking for keen young men and women to join the staff. The depot, started by Pickston and about thirty key employees from the Handley Page parent company at Cricklewood, London, went on to employ some 3,000 people.

Halifax front and rear fuselage repair hangar. YARD, Rawcliffe.

I duly travelled to the City of York in, I think, the spring of 1942. I was billeted on the edge of the airfield, and obviously the Luftwaffe heard of my arrival and attacked both the airfield and the city. My appointment at the YARD was like a dream come true, although I have to admit that I was overawed by the immense size of the aeroplanes when I was first shown round the depot. Happy though I was at Rawcliffe, at the age of seventeen I volunteered for aircrew but was informed that I'd have to wait another year.

Some short time later, I was sent for by the boss, who had been told that I had volunteered to join the RAF. He went on to explain that with five different companies manufacturing the Halifax at widely dispersed sites, from Liverpool in the north to the

Assembly hangars at YARD, Water Lane.

Handley Page assembly at their airfield in Radlett, Hertfordshire, and with each aeroplane having to be test flown before delivery to the various RAF stations, the demand for pilots and flight engineers was considerable. Whilst a number of mature test pilots, both civilian and RAF, were available, the role of flight engineer was a new one concerning the four-engined aeroplanes. Handley Page at the YARD would have to provide their own test flight crews; in fact this would be the case at each of the five factories making the Halifax. And so he proposed that I should withdraw my application to join the RAF and go to Radlett for flying training, after which I would return to York. Not unnaturally, as a mere seventeen-year-old, this was a very attractive proposition and one which I quickly accepted.

Typical Halifax on production test flight from Clifton, York.

As a point of interest to historians, in all there were approximately 10,000 individual Halifax test flights, including those at York. And to the best of my knowledge, whilst there were many 'incidents' none involved fatalities. Incidentally, each new or re-built aeroplane was test flown to a very strict procedure, including maximum speed dives, stalls, performance checks with feathered airscrews, brake tests, etc., with each flight taking about an hour.

Having accepted Eric Pickston's offer, one of my first jobs was to set up a flight office at the Water Lane site. I was instructed to obtain, from a firm in London (I think it was D. Lewis and Sons), both pilots' and flight engineers' overalls – white for the pilots and royal blue for the flight engineers. In addition, I ordered from the RAF six parachute

Nineteen-year-old author ready for take-off in Halifax LW477, March 1945.

harnesses and ten parachute chest-type packs, together with various sizes of flying boots. For a young lad, such responsibility felt great. Furthermore, I had to organise with RAF Church Fenton, to 'hang' the parachutes on a monthly basis, each canopy having its own log book for recording the procedure, and I had many enjoyable trips to Church Fenton taking in time-expired parachutes and collecting the 'hung' ones. Finally, I was told to obtain leather flying helmets complete with oxygen masks and intercom equipment. I had well and truly 'arrived'.

I was always driven to Church Fenton in a small Hillman pick-up truck and thoroughly enjoyed myself. The driver was either Hilda Cleminson or Sonia Royle. Apart from her general driving duties, Hilda spent many hours sitting on the airfield in a Hillman or Austin ambulance. This was simply a covered pick-up with a red cross on the side and had we had an accident there wouldn't have been much room for bodies. Fortunately, it was never put to the test.

The procedure for me and for the pilots was that we recorded each and every air test. These reports were signed and handed over to the aeronautical inspection department

Parachutes hanging, pre packing.

(AID) who had several officers based on site. For my first Halifax test flight before going to Radlett, I flew as passenger with an RAF pilot and flight engineer; the noise and vibration shattered me beyond belief.

A most interesting aspect of our flying at Clifton Moor was if and when 4 Group or 6 Group reported a 'rogue' Halifax on one of the squadrons. These were aeroplanes that were constantly being reported as 'unserviceable' and early returns, i.e. those which had set off on a sortie and had returned to base early because of a problem. The pilot and I would fly to the station concerned (we had an Airspeed Oxford for this purpose) and then fly the offending aeroplane to our standard procedure, submitting a report to the squadron engineering officer on our findings. I should perhaps add, in all fairness, that most of the offending aeroplanes were based at the heavy conversion units at Rufforth and Marston Moor. Nearly all the aeroplanes used at these units were ex-Bomber Command and were inevitably 'tired'.

Production test flying at Clifton involved, over a five-year period, all marks of Halifax including those with Rolls-Royce engines and the later marks with Bristol Hercules engines, including Mark IXs. This latter type proved to be far superior in all respects: better rate of climb, better cruising performance, and an all round better aeroplane. Incidents at Clifton were infrequent and mainly concerned airframe and engine adjustments. Not untypical was an incident when the dinghy cover located on the port inner wing became detached and hit the tailplane as we were taking off, luckily with no damage to the tailplane, or to the crew. Engine failure was not uncommon and in one instance whilst landing into a cross-wind on three engines, a flock of plovers decided to take off and the so-called bullet-proof second pilot's windscreen was shattered, leaving me covered in blood and feathers. It was many months before the pilot, Sandy, or I could face chicken for lunch. The Halifax involved was C VII G-AITC (PP320) which was subsequently used on the Berlin Airlift.

I had a closer brush with death whilst flying a Halifax Mk III MZ506 at the Handley Page repair depot in August 1944. However I was blissfully unaware of it until forty years later. I was with Jimmy Talbot as pilot and he had developed a habit of 'feeling' the ailerons (to determine

Halifax C VII G-AITC PP320. A converted bomber used on the Berlin Airlift. Modified and air tested at Clifton airfield, York, 1945. (Author 2nd pilot.)

Date.	Aircraft.		Engines.		Journey.	
	Type.	Markings.	Type.	H.P.	From.	To.
						Brought forwa
18.11.47.	HALIFAX A VII	PN308 ✓	BRISTOL ④ HERCULES XVI	1.650.	YORK .	YORK .
18.11.47.	"	NA407. ✓	"	"	"	"
24.11.47.	" "	NA 407.	"	"	"	"
25.11.47 .	" CVIII	G-AITC. PP320	"	1.100's ④	(CIVIL AIRCRAFT).	"
26.11.4).	" C VIII	PP320	"	"	"	"
26.11.47)	" C VIII	"	"	"	YORK	RADLETT
9.12.47	" A VII	PN251 ; Bristol Herc. X VI	"	"	"	York
9.12.47)	" "	PN251 .	"	"	"	York .
						Carried forward

| RECORD O|

Detail from the author's post-war record of flights.

whether they were light or heavy) when we reached a height of about 100 feet. On this particular flight he carried out his usual procedure and then said very abruptly that we were returning to base immediately. I never saw his pilot's report and mine was obviously very brief, saying something similar to 'flight aborted'.

It was only explained when I welcomed to the museum Jack Crane, who was second-in-charge to Charlie Carpenter in the flight preparation hangar at YARD. They were two very competent aviation engineers, and it was a great pleasure to see Jack again after so many years. After a great deal of reminiscing he told me I was very lucky to be alive and running the Yorkshire Air Museum. I was baffled until he explained that on the flight in question we'd almost suffered aileron over-balance and that we had been within seconds of a catastrophic failure, it was only because of the extremely skilful piloting that we had even survived. Tragically it was elevator over-balance that caused Jimmy's death in the prototype Handley Page Hermes at Radlett in December 1945. Thus I never had a chance to thank him.

By the time World War Two was declared the concept of aviation was less than forty years old. Flying between 1919 and 1939 had obviously advanced by leaps and bounds, but with typical government hesitation, technological development only really started in the 1930s. By mid-1943 the Vale of York had become almost like a land-based aircraft carrier. From the north, near Darlington, to the south of the county at Finningley, military airfields sprang up like mushrooms and were planned to accommodate the new four-engined bombers. Apart from

FLIGHTS.

Time of Departure.		Time of Arrival.		Time in Air.		Pilot. See Instructions (5) & (6) on flyleaf of this book.	Remarks.		
Hrs.	Mins.	Hrs.	Mins.	Hrs.	Mins.				
...	...	...	...	217	15.				R.A.F.
	20.	13	00		40.	F/L. ALLUM .	H.P. Test Flight	F/Engineer	Test Pilot.
	8c	15	00		30.	"	"	"	" "
	25	12	45		20	"	"	(CAME IN ON 3 ENGINES) (BIRD HIT WINDSCREEN.)	
	35	12	65		30.	Mr. W.G. SANDERS .	"		
	30	11	40		10	"	"		
	50	15	35		45	"	DELIVERY TO H.P. RADLETT.		
	00	12	35		35	S/L. Hazeldan Chief Test Pilot	H.P.	F/Engineer	Test flight
	25	1	35		10.	"	"	"	"
	...	...	...	220	55.				

the requisitioning of the land, the actual building was an enormous undertaking. Concrete runways and perimeter tracks of something like three miles, plus hangars (although not all had hangarage), Nissen huts for officers, airmen and WAAFs, at least three separate ablution blocks, offices, storerooms and no doubt several other facilities I can't now think of. All this from a civil engineering point of view was a tremendous achievement, especially considering that about twenty-five of them were built. I wonder how long the process would take nowadays.

With the expansion and development of Bomber Command, two groups were established: 4 Group with headquarters at Heslington Hall in York, and 6 Group with their headquarters at Allerton Park, near Knaresborough. By 1943 all the airfields were equipped with four-engined types, mainly Halifaxes. These new large bombers with all-up weights of 30 tons were technologically advanced on the previous types used by the RAF. However there was a distinct lack of experience of flying these large aeroplanes with a 100 foot wingspan, whose engines collectively would develop over 5,000 brake horse power. For example, on take-off with the rotation of each engine in the same direction there was tremendous torque, which would cause them to swing violently. As a result, and with newly recruited twenty-year-old pilots learning to control these monsters, crashes were frequent.

With so many active airfields within a radius of forty miles of the City of York and considering that there would be at least one or two squadrons per airfield, it was quite common to hear and see 300 to 400 aeroplanes in the skies above the York landscape, and, to

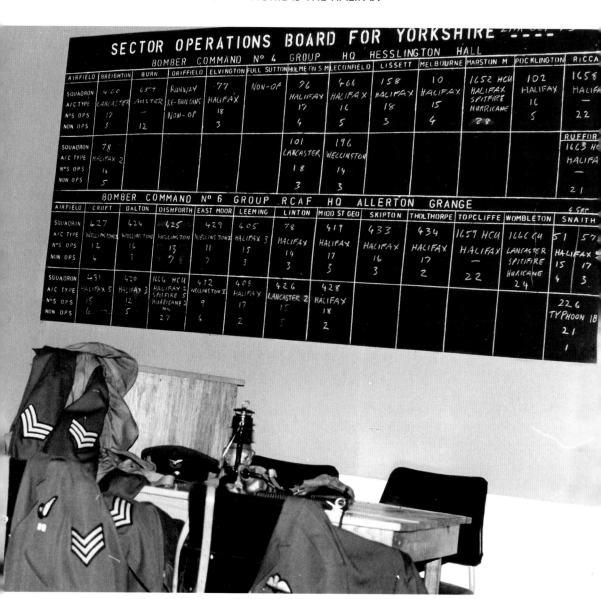

Ops board: 4 Group RAF and 6 Group RCAF.

those of us who witnessed this huge armada, it seemed sad that such historic events were being forgotten; especially considering some 55,673 aircrew, over 18,000 (nearly a third) from Yorkshire bases, were killed or missing from Bomber Command's actions. It was for this reason that the writer and several hundred other people set about creating the Yorkshire Air Museum as a memorial to those courageous young men.

CHAPTER 2 YARD to YAM

HALIFAX PRODUCTION

My involvement with YAM rekindled happy memories of my war-time years at YARD, where my admiration and affection for the Handley Page Halifax began.

Between the two world wars, the Air Ministry drew up specifications for the manufacture of all-metal, twin-engined heavy bombers, and in 1937 several British companies were invited to tender. The specification, typically bureaucratic, called for aeroplanes that would carry paratroops and tow gliders, and to be equipped with powered gun turrets, utilising 0.303 machine guns. Several companies were involved in tendering and these of course included Handley Page, with headquarters at Claremont Road, Cricklewood in London. Mr. Frederick Handley Page (as he was at that time) with his chief designers, approached the Air Ministry with a proposal that the aeroplane should be designed minus the gun turrets, as a high speed, high altitude machine. His theory was to outfly any enemy defences, both anti-aircraft guns and fighters.

His proposals were rejected. How typically short-sighted, when one bears in mind that one of the most successful aeroplanes manufactured during World War Two was, of course, the de Havilland Mosquito which acted in all attack and defence roles – minus gun turrets.

Of the companies who tendered to the 1937 specification, Handley Page, Short Brothers, and A.V. Roe were successful. Typical of Air Ministry indecision, the original Halifax was planned on paper to use twin Rolls-Royce Vulture engines, which ultimately proved rather unsuccessful. It was then decided that the Halifax would be built with four Rolls-Royce Merlin 10s, although Handley Page expressed the opinion that it would be more successful if fitted with Bristol Hercules radials. The aeroplane was to be fitted with a retractable undercarriage and have an all-up weight of 66,000 lbs, an increase of nearly six tons, using the original airframe – a very good reflection on the basic strength of the original concept. The first prototype was flown by Major J.L. Cordes and E.A. 'Ginger' Wright, on 25th October 1939, from RAF Bicester, near Oxford, which was a remarkable feat since the specification had only been drawn up in 1937.

Between 1940 and 1945 over 6,000 of the type were produced and used in each and every RAF Command with the exception of Fighter Command. It was the only British four-engined bomber used in the Middle East, where it acted both in its bomber role and as a glider tower

Halifaxes in formation.

(it was the only RAF type capable of towing the huge Hamilcar glider). In 1945 it was used in the Far East and because of its air-cooled engines it proved suitable, whereas the Lancaster, with its liquid-cooled engines operated with great difficulty. How could one fail to be impressed by such an aeroplane?

My arrival at Elvington triggered other happy memories. I met my first wife, Jess Silk, under the wing of a Halifax at the YARD and we spent fifty, very happy, years together. The Halifax also became an introduction later when in 1998 and after I'd lost Jess, a lady telephoned YAM and told me that she had worked at the YARD during the war and suggested that as it was fifty years since the depot closed, it might be a good idea for us to organise a reunion. To cut a long story short, I responded to her phone call by dropping in to see her. And the following year we were married. How remarkable that an aeroplane could play such an important and happy part in my life.

THE BIRTH OF THE YORKSHIRE AIR MUSEUM

Before we had formed the trust at the museum, a number of us gathered initially at Rachel Semlyen's house, Brinkworth Park, and people came from all walks of life, including some young aviation enthusiasts. Two in particular were Chris Dunham and Mark Lewis. Chris was a computer engineer and it was he who compiled the first membership list on computer, i.e. the names and addresses of the many people who were willing and keen to join us.

Jess and Ian. First 'Halifax marriage' of fifty years.

Second 'Halifax marriage', Ian and Mary in 1998.

Our first member was not from Bomber Command but in fact flew Spitfires and came to England as part of the Free French contingency. He was Capitaine Gabriel (known as 'Gabby') Calcagni and he was extremely enthusiastic about our ideas, hence he was the first to pay his membership fee. He struck up a friendship with myself and with Ian Wormald, who at the time was still serving as a squadron leader in the RAF. Ian arranged for Gabby to join him on a flight in a Jet Provost from Leeming. Gabby learned of Elvington's close association with the French air force in 1944 and from then on he acted as interpreter when the Bombardier Lourds (heavy bomber) team visited YAM. I don't know why he was not invited to become a trustee. He returned to his home in France after the war, but found the political in-fighting unacceptable and came back to England, to set up a business in Darlington.

Mark Dunham was part of a group of young people, referred to as 'wreckologists', whose hobby was to track down known World War Two crash sites with a view to researching the incidents and, with the help of metal detectors, discovering parts of aeroplane. I was particularly pleased when these youngsters were keen to learn from me about the history of the Halifax in Yorkshire, and it was Mark who told me that in the Outer Hebrides was a 20 foot section of a Halifax fuselage which was being used as a hen hut and had been there for many years. This information whetted my appetite and with his help I found the name of the farmer who owned it. How then was I to contact Mr. MacKenzie? When I tried, I found that most of the people who live on the Isle of Lewis are called MacKenzie! In the finish, I simply wrote to Mr. Norman MacKenzie c/o the Isle of Lewis, and I was delighted when he wrote back saying we could have the hut/fuselage with pleasure. The story then really began. How do you transport a big lump of old aeroplane some 500 miles, including a sea journey?

In 1983 I was chairman of the parish council in my home village of Scotton, near Knaresborough and I was called on from time to time to attend social events. On one such occasion I was introduced to a retired RAF group captain, Bill Hickey.

During idle conversation I told him of our plans for an air museum at Elvington and also of our

Our first member: Capitaine Gabriel Calcagni with his Spitfire in 1944.

The hen hut near Stornoway.

Farmer MacKenzie and his hen hut in 1984.

Ian Wormwald and Gabby after their flight in a Jet Provost.

interest in part of a Halifax on the Isle of Lewis. Unbeknown to me, Bill later contacted an ex-colleague of his, Air Chief Marshal Sir Michael Knight, who was at that time serving as air member for supply and organisation on the Air Force Board at the Ministry of Defence. Sir Michael told Bill that they were carrying out lifting operations on the Outer Hebrides, using Chinook helicopters and said that if we could locate the item we required the RAF would be pleased to assist as part of their training exercise. What a stroke of luck. With a lot more to come.

A few days later my wife Jess rang me at the office (I was still fully employed at that time) with a message from RAF Finningley saying that if I could be at the base early the following morning, the RAF would fly me to the Outer Hebrides to organise this important action. This message came as a complete

Group Captain Bill Hickey.

surprise and unfortunately I had an important appointment at our head office in London the following day, one I couldn't miss. In my place stepped a serving navigator, a flight lieutenant (later a squadron leader) who offered to join the flight, investigate the scene, take masses of photographs, and also to make contact with the Chinook crews on site. This gentleman was the extremely well-known Flight Lieutenant Burgess, known throughout the RAF as 'Budgie' – and who was steeped in the history of the RAF. His father was a pilot who flew one of the three famous Gladiators on the island of Malta during the war: Faith, Hope and Charity. Budgie became one of our keenest YAM supporters, and in future years he was to arrange many of the important fly-pasts which took place at Elvington. Incidentally, I was more than a little taken aback by the photos he brought back from Lewis.

At this stage in the development of what was to become generally known as the 'Halifax project', my aim was to retrieve, restore and display this important part of a World War Two Halifax at Elvington when we had somewhere to work on it.

THE FIRST BITS OF THE JIGSAW

To return to the hen hut, when Budgie got back he reported on his very thorough and painstaking investigations on the island, and explained that it would not be just a simple matter of air-lifting the fuselage section, a lot of work would have to be done before it could be dug out. How then did I, sat in an office in Leeds, try to organise such an undertaking? First of all, Mark Lewis offered to transport himself to the islands and then I was put in touch with the air training corps squadron based at Stornoway. The telephone lines between Leeds and Stornoway became somewhat heated when it was suggested that another member of the MacKenzie family had offered to use his JCB mechanical digger to remove a considerable amount of earth into which the fuselage had settled.

To add further to the complications, the Chinook crews had located from the air *another* crash site which contained several Merlin engines and a complete tailwheel assembly, again from a Halifax. Before we could do anything about recovering any of these parts, I had to get permission from the Ministry of Defence by giving precise details of the individual aeroplane which had crashed into mountains. It lay south-west of the Tarbet Gap, frequently used by the Coastal Command Halifaxes of 58 Squadron as a short-cut on their return to Stornoway after carrying out surveillance operations over the Atlantic. Our investigations revealed that the Mk II JP165 (which had been manufactured by the London Passenger Transport Board) had hit the mountainside on 9th April 1945.

A sequel to this research was that I received a phone call from a relative of a member of the crew of JP165, who was tragically killed in the crash. I was asked if we could throw some light on the incident. From previous experience involving similar investigations, I was never too keen to pass on detailed information. Sadly, the official report suggested that the crash had been caused because of poor navigation. And who was the navigator? The husband of the lady on whose behalf the enquiries had been made. It goes without saying that she was extremely upset – a situation which I'd tried to avoid.

Halifax 710. The last bomber built by London Passenger Transport at Leavesdon.

Halifax GR Mk II JP165 of 58 Squadron crashed on the Isle of Harris, 9th April 1945. The RAF collected Merlin engines via helicopter, one engine was rebuilt at YAM.

The engines and tailwheel assembly from JP165 were well and truly embedded in soft peat on the mountainside, and as in the case of the fuselage, the Chinook boys could not attempt to airlift these items without them first being dug out. My next job then was to obtain permission from the landowners for the rescue crew to gain access. After Mr. MacKenzie (the second) had used his JCB to good effect, the Chinook lifted the engines and the tailwheel assembly to Stornoway airfield.

So far so good, but how did we transport all these bits and pieces to Elvington? Fortunately, one of my drivers, Ray Bainbridge, at the Leeds factory had heard the story to date and volunteered his services free of charge, providing I would give permission for him to use one of the company's trucks. This I was happy to do and together with his son and a friend they set off on a trip of about 1,000 miles. As part of the journey involved a sea crossing, I then contacted the ferry company, Caledonian MacBrayne explaining our problem, asking for their help. They came up trumps, taking the vehicle and its load free of charge.

Due to the hive of activity on what had previously been the sleepy Isle of Lewis, the locals were intrigued and our exploits generated a lot of publicity, for Caledonian MacBrayne and for YAM. The goings-on became headline news in the *Stornoway Gazette* and the news eventually travelled to Glasgow, where we made it to the local news.

Before our vehicle left Leeds, we had manufactured a special cradle as we suspected that the fuselage would be in a

Restored fuselage, HR792 Halifax returns, 1989.

33

pretty fragile state and with the project to raise and conserve the Tudor warship the *Mary Rose* in mind we didn't want to risk any damage to this fifty–year-old piece of aeroplane. A few days after I'd been told that the load had left Stornoway, I was awakened at 5 a.m. on a lovely summer morning to find our vehicle outside my home in Scotton with one large piece of Halifax fuselage on board. It was a memorable and moving moment, I must confess.

We then planned for the vehicle to be driven to Elvington where Rachel had arranged a reception party, which included the Earl and Countess of Halifax. It was the Earl's grandmother who had named the first production example, L9485, at Radlett in 1941. Also present were two of the flight commanders who had been based at Elvington during the war: Wing Commanders Bobby Sage and 'Butch' Surtees, and another Halifax pilot who flew with 10 Squadron, Bob Halstead. Bob and his cousin Ron Pfertner were to become regular visitors and supporters at YAM and have also become valued friends.

Throughout my many happy years at Elvington, the late Wing Commander R.J. Sage, OBE, AFC, was I think, my most loyal and encouraging supporter. During his distinguished career in the RAF, Robert was selected to assist in a most secret operation to identify the directional beams used by the Germans to pin-point their targets. A young scientist, R.V. Jones, aged twenty-one, was convinced that the Germans were using this facility. Few senior officers believed this to be true, but the story came to Churchill's attention and he insisted that the matter be investigated.

Hen hut arrives at Elvington, 1984, ex HR792 Halifax.

Robert Sage was one of two pilots selected, along with a wireless operator and a specially-adapted radio to cruise the east coast and attempt to confirm or deny that this beam system existed. They had to fly in all weathers, at night, and eventually were able to confirm that R.V. Jones was absolutely right. The photo on page 35 shows Robert delivering this very special radio to Elvington.

Robert was a tremendous asset to the Yorkshire Air Museum and devoted a lot of time and energy into getting things under way. There were many times when I had to apologise to his dear wife Peggy for keeping

L to R: Wing Commander Surtees, unknown, Wing Commander Sage, Rachel Semlyen and author.

him so long away from home. He was a Halifax pilot with 77 Squadron based at Elvington when on 9th March 1943, he was shot down and spent the rest of the war in a prisoner-of-war camp. Robert's own account of the incident, together with the official report from Flt Lt Barker, the navigator is documented in appendices 1 and 2 of this book. The photograph of the badly damaged aeroplane was taken by a member of the resistance.

Robert 'Bobby' Sage with the unique radio used to identify German beams.

One of the many interesting incidents at the museum involved the brother and nephew of a member of 77 Squadron who had been shot down on the same night as Bobby, I think their name was Huggard. Apparently, the body of the missing brother had never been located and they fully expected that Robert could shed some light

Robert Sage's crashed Halifax DT 734 of 77 Squadron, Elvington. Downed during a raid on Munich, 9th/10th March 1943.

Wing Commander Robert Sage OBE AFC, president of YAM, in a pensive mood with the former hen hut.

on the incident. Each year they visited YAM in the hope that we had been able to find out more. Sure enough, the story had a happy conclusion when one of our members, Bill Hird, a former 77 Squadron member, was on holiday near Lake Constance, which lies between Germany and Switzerland. He met some local people who told him of their efforts to pull the remains of a Halifax out of the lake. Bill made a lot of enquiries and astonishingly it turned out to be the missing Halifax from 77 Squadron which had crashed and submerged into the lake on that fateful night. Needless to say, the Huggards were so relieved to know at last where their relative had been lost – yet another YAM story with a happy ending.

LUCK WAS ON OUR SIDE

At this time, YAM was in its infancy and one of our major problems was where to store the bits and pieces, when yet again Bobby Sage came up with a solution. As he was at one time the commanding officer at RAF Dishforth, he approached the incumbent CO, who readily agreed to provide a lockable garage where we placed the Halifax fuselage. This made it possible for Bobby and me to visit the site at weekends with a view to cleaning down the airframe which had several tons of Scottish peat sticking to it.

This also gave me the opportunity to find out the origins and history of the aeroplane, which turned out to be HR792. Produced at Radlett in 1943, it had been collected by an air transport auxiliary pilot, Lettice Curtis, who flew it to Cunliffe Owen for conversion to Coastal Command requirements, and then finally it was transferred to 58 Squadron, RAF.

Having got the fuselage into store at Dishforth, we had three Merlin engines to accommodate and rather than place them in the still derelict buildings at Elvington, a close friend of mine, George Pickard, a director of Vibroplant Limited of Harrogate, suggested that they could be placed in their engineering workshop. This proved to be an excellent move as one of Vibroplant's engineers, Jim Garnet, offered to try to restore one of the three. It surprised us all when the rocker covers and sump cover were removed that the engines were in remarkably good condition. The oil had lubricated everything when the aeroplane crashed. Jim reassembled the one engine which, after several years' work that is, went on display at Elvington. And after I'd managed to scrounge some electric motors the engine could be seen turning (obviously at very low revs) for the public to enjoy. Alongside the Rolls-Royce engine was a sectionalised Bristol Hercules air-cooled radial of the type fitted to the later marks of Halifax. Again, this was fitted with an electric motor and many visitors, including ex-RAF people who'd flown them, were intrigued to see how sleeve valves of the Hercules functioned.

I recall so clearly an occasion when Bobby Sage and I met at Dishforth, trying to make the fuselage look respectable; he said to me: "Having achieved this bit, Ian, where on earth do we go from here?" I then had to admit that I'd already taken the next step and had made an appointment for both of us to visit Mike Edwards, who was at that time director and general manager at British Aerospace of Brough, near Hull. It was my intention to ask if he had any ideas on the restoration of the fuselage section. On our arrival, Michael showed us the magnificent office where Robert Blackburn had carried out so much of his work. We were then taken down to the superbly equipped apprentices' section, which was fitted out with about thirty work-benches, smartly dressed apprentices, and mature and hospitable instructors. Michael then offered his idea to the instructors and to Robert and me, saying that it would be an excellent training scheme to bring the fuselage section for restoration by the apprentices. I couldn't believe my ears, I was like a child with a new toy!

With all this help and enthusiasm it was at about this time that I began to think we should do more than display the various parts of a Halifax, could we possibly recover enough parts to do a complete rebuild? We had after all got the main piece – the fuselage – and the news of our endeavours seemed to be spreading like wildfire, with help coming from all directions. The whole thing seemed to be gathering momentum and I have to admit that at times it seemed overwhelming. But I decided, yes, it could be done! When I voiced my thoughts it was Bob Halstead who said: "I admire your enthusiasm, Ian, but I can't see you completing a full-sized example of a Halifax."

There was a very big snag, however, and that was the complete lack of Handley Page drawings. Having heard Mike Edwards' tremendous idea, I felt that somehow or other, by hook or by crook, I had to do something. So I sought help from the Handley Page Association, a group formed by Handley Page employees, and I contacted the chairman, Harry Fraser-Mitchell, a retired member of the design team.

The late Flight Lieutenant Bob Halstead RAF DFC, 10 Squadron.

It transpired that Harry still had links with Handley Page after the company had been put into receivership when the Ministry of Defence failed to place further orders for Victors. Handley Page Ltd went into voluntary liquidation on 8th August 1969 and re-structuring confirmed that the contract for conversion of 18 Victors to K.2 standard would hold. A new company, Handley Page Aircraft Ltd, was formed in November 1969, but was wound up in February 1970, and the Ministry of Defence moved the contract for Victors to Hawker Siddeley in April 1970. Obviously, the receivers were only interested in the fixed assets, and instructed staff to destroy the many thousands of drawings, but we, of course, were only interested in those relating to all marks of Halifax. Fortunately for us, Harry had thought at the time that this was a crime, especially from a historical point of view, and he contacted the Imperial War Museum, who agreed to store the drawings at Duxford, near Cambridge. Consequently, when Harry heard of our project at Brough we arranged to meet at Duxford with a view to retrieving the relevant drawings for our project. The IWM had no objection providing that BAe would micro-fiche and return same for ease of storage. This was yet another happy outcome for Robert, and for me, and I recall him saying, as he was to say many more times over the next few years, "Luck is on your side, Ian". Little did he realise there was more good fortune coming quite quickly.

BAe apprentices restoring Halifax HR792 fuselage, 1986-7, Brough, East Yorkshire.

Once the drawings arrived at Brough, the apprentices became fully occupied with what to them and their instructors became a fascinating project. I vividly remember the expressions on the faces of the workers at Brough when we transported this fifty-year-old piece of aeroplane into the factory, where dozens of Hawk jet trainers were being built. For the next year or so, at the invitation of BAe, Robert and I would visit Brough to inspect the work in progress, and our visits created a most friendly and hospitable attitude from all those involved. I think what intrigued them most was the sight of these two grey-haired old aviators showing such enthusiasm. I really think that we appeared to them as being from the 'Red Baron' era of World War One, particularly when Robert told them that his first flying experience had been at the flying school operated by Blackburns in the 1930s. It transpired that Robert had learned to fly in Blackburn B2 G-AEBJ, and that the actual aeroplane still existed at Brough – and in airworthy condition. When I told them that my first flight had been in an Avro 504K in 1935 at Skipton, North Yorkshire, at a cost of five shillings, the picture was complete.

I should add at this stage that the major breakthrough in the creation of our Halifax was due to the foresight and work of both Harry Fraser-Mitchell and his wife, Rosamund. Little did we realise at this stage that once work on the fuselage had been completed, the same apprentices with Mike Edwards' approval, would manufacture a completely new rear bay which carried the rear turret, tailplane, and tailwheel assembly. Finally, if these drawings had not become available, I doubt if the whole project would have progressed.

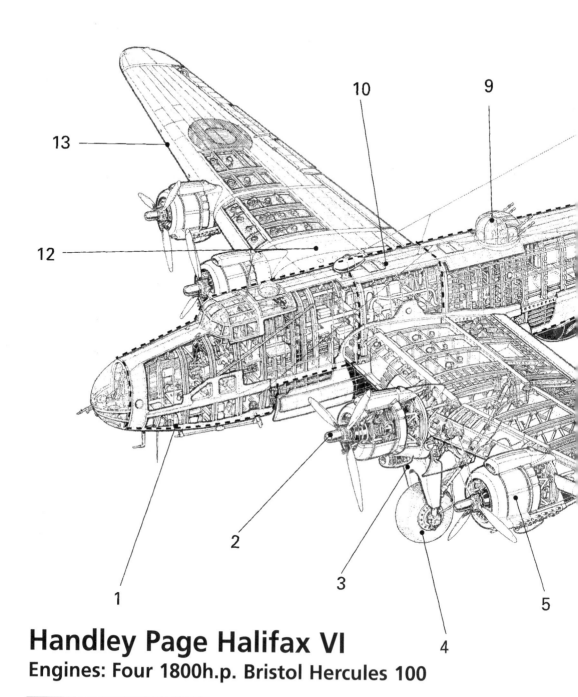

Handley Page Halifax VI

Engines: Four 1800h.p. Bristol Hercules 100

Dimensions of Halifax Mark III		
Wing Span	Height	Length
104ft 0ins	21ft 4ins	71ft 7ins

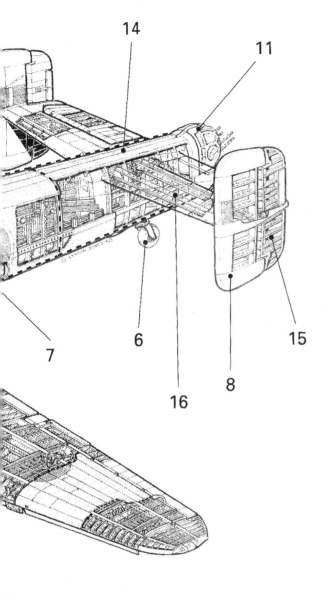

14

11

7

6

16

8

15

KEY TO SCHEMATIC DIAGRAM – WHERE ALL THE PARTS CAME FROM

No	Sub Assembly	Source
1	Front fuselage section	Built by YAM volunteers from scratch, using original Handley Page drawings.
2	Propeller Hubs	From Halifax LW687, 432 Sqn RCAF, shot down 31/3/44, raid on Nuremburg.
3	Undercarriage Legs	Manufactured from new by the late John Wilkinson of Pudsey.
4	Main Landing Wheels	Ex Halifax, details unknown.
5	Engines: Bristol Hercules	French air force and Groupes Lourds.
6	Tail Wheel	From Halifax HX271, 466 Sqn RAAF, shot down 3/6/44.
7	Rear Fuselage Assembly	From Halifax HR792, 58 Sqn RAF, crashed Stornoway 13/1/45.
8	Tail Fins	Manufactured from new by BAe (Brough).
9	Mid-Upper Turret	Unknown Halifax – ex garden cloche.
10	'Covered Wagon' Fuselage Section	Unknown Linton-on-Ouse Halifax.
11	Rear Turret	Unknown Halifax; restored by Bernard Jefferson.
12	Centre Section and Intermediate Wings	From Handley Page Hastings TG536 at RAF Catterick.
13	Outer Mainplanes	From another Hastings – unused, as new.
14	Rear Bay	Manufactured from new by BAe (Brough) from original Handley Page drawings.
15	Rudders	Manufactured from new by volunteers at YAM, using original Handley Page drawings.
16	Tail Plane	Partly from Halifax LL505, crashed Lake District 22/10/44; part built from scratch by YAM volunteers.

A HOME FOR THE HALIFAX

With all this enthusiasm for the Halifax project, it was essential that I should concentrate my efforts on getting YAM onto a more established footing. It was thus vital that we should get some of the derelict buildings restored. Following on from Rachel's original idea and from the publicity she generated, many interested (and interesting) people, young and old and from all walks of life and all corners of the county and beyond, volunteered their services. About seven buildings still existed in the area which she was particularly keen to preserve, on something like six acres, but the land and the buildings were in a very sorry state. Overgrown with weeds of every description, it was a very sad sight and an extremely daunting prospect. Neglected for many years, buildings which had been intended to be 'temporary' had survived for half a century, but only just.

The flying control tower, the very heart of wartime airfields, still existed and attracted our first efforts. Built partly as 'bomb-proof', i.e. the walls were three bricks thick without a cavity, and because they were externally cement rendered, the moisture easily tracked through to the inside of the building. All the window frames were metal and very badly corroded and took a tremendous amount of time and effort by hundreds of volunteers to restore. But it was such an important and valuable asset. And so began fifteen years of very hard, interesting and rewarding work in helping to create what is now YAM. Our main aim was to make the site a

Early days at YAM.

Planning the future while sitting on a Hastings wing. L to R: Fawcett, Pontefract, Semlyen, author, Dunham.

memorial to the thousands of men and women who had served their country from all the bases in Yorkshire, and our thoughts were also of all those who came from Commonwealth countries, and from France, North America, Norway and Poland. The name 'Yorkshire Air Museum' was suggested, but at that time I was not particularly keen on the word 'museum' and would have preferred perhaps Yorkshire Aviation Heritage, but on the other hand 'yam' is an old Yorkshire dialect word for 'home' so it is quite fitting after all. Thus the Yorkshire Air Museum and Allied Air Forces Memorial was decided upon.

Before we had even registered as a charity, Rachel approached Jack Birch, chairman of the company William Birch and Sons who owned the site at Elvington, and he very generously agreed that we could take over the first two acres on a rental basis. Later, the site was extended to about six acres and again with the help and co-operation of the Birch family and with grant aid, the land was purchased at a nominal price. Jack Birch was to become one of our life-long supporters. The late Squadron Leader Jim Donaldson, at the time chairman of North Yorkshire County Council, played a major role in the granting of charity status.

We took over a totally derelict site – the buildings were windowless and doorless and some were minus their roofs. One of our early projects was to convert the ablutions block into a small NAAFI type cafe. I was still a director at that time of a company in the Cookson Group, and whilst at a meeting in London I met the managing director of Valspar Limited, paint manufacturers who were also part of the group. I told him of our project at Elvington and jokingly asked him if they ever had any 'second-hand' paint. Much to my surprise, he offered

Building the Handley Page hangar.

me several hundred litres of an emulsion which was no longer fashionable, and he delivered it free of charge. Needless to say, most of the interiors of everything we renovated were painted in an unfashionable but very acceptable shade of cream. Later on the NAAFI building was trebled in size, the work being carried out by the Youth Training Scheme. This scheme, now defunct, was an effort to get thousands of young people into employment. But some of them had a bit of a past and on one occasion the YTS management asked if I could get the local press to take a photograph for use with an article on the scheme, showing the team in action. Dutifully, I asked them all to take up certain positions on what was then the new NAAFI building and invited the photographer to join me. But, surprise surprise! They had all disappeared. I wonder why?

One of the problems we had when we first started the museum was that we didn't have large enough buildings to house the aeroplanes, or even bits of them, and by then we had already started on the Halifax project. We heard about a structure that was for sale at Selby, a building owned if I remember rightly by British Oil and Cake Mills. Ted Fawcett and I went to have a look at it. Really, what was for sale was the steelwork, and so we made an offer (in the region of £2,000 I suppose). We were struggling to raise that sort of money in those days. Nevertheless, we purchased it and Ted obtained planning permission. Ted, being an architect, designed buildings and submitted plans to the local authority, which in those days was Selby District Council. He had been a Halifax pilot with, I think, 298 Squadron flying 'special duties', in supporting clandestine operations. What a valuable job he did for us at YAM also.

After many months of work, we finally completed what we called the Handley Page Building, again with the help of the YTS. Incidentally, these boys were not paid by us and the only cost to the museum was their daily transport. Missing from the bits we had, were the main doors, but with another stroke of good fortune Tony Pickard, with the help of Arnold Burton, discovered that building contractors were about to dismantle Wetherby bus station, and surplus to requirements were huge metal-framed doors complete with running equipment, worth many thousands of pounds. The contractors agreed to give this equipment to YAM and with a lot of effort from Tony and the YTS boys, the doors were fitted, thus allowing us to move the partly-built Halifax in and out of its new home. Once the building was completed Group Captain Tom Eeles, commanding officer at Linton-on-Ouse, carried out the official opening and unveiled a plaque commemorating the event.

During the 1980s the lottery fund was established, and I felt that the organisation may look favourably at a request from us to fund the erection of a World War Two T2 hangar. The procedures were new and we felt we had nothing to lose in approaching them, as we already had on site the basic structure for such a building which we'd purchased second-hand. The late Ron Pontefract and I, having obtained the masses of application forms, started the lengthy task of completing them. The questions asked beggared belief. Nevertheless, after many head-scratching hours, we completed and submitted them to lottery headquarters who asked for the name of a contact at the museum, and mine was given.

For many, many weeks following I had frequent telephone conversations with a young lady who was handling our application in a London office. Not unnaturally, I used to receive lots of calls about the museum at home, and on one memorable day my wife Jess greeted me with a larger than usual smile and told me that an important telephone call from the lottery was imminent. To my delight, the young lady duly rang and told me that we had been given a grant of £124,000, but she was quick to remind me that we at YAM must raise an equivalent amount and the grant was conditional on such action on our part.

Naively, I thought we would then be presented with a cheque for the total, but oh dear no! The wheels of bureaucracy move very slowly and it was explained to us that we could only make claims from the fund after each stage had been completed, in other words, a contractor would do the work, invoice the museum, and expect payment, but of course we couldn't pay him until we'd claimed that amount from the lottery fund. Fortunately, one of my colleagues and a fellow trustee, John Wilkins, was a civil engineer by profession and from then on he made things much easier for us by getting the money flowing a little more quickly. After completion of the T2 hangar we estimated the total cost at £250,000 and so we at the museum had to raise the other £126,000. A daunting task. But once again, we received tremendous support, not least from Doug Sample of the Canadian branch, who raised about £30,000. We were also granted some £20,000 from PRISM, a fund for the preservation of industrial and scientific

T2 hangar under construction.

THE
CANADIAN
MEMORIAL HANGAR

DEDICATED TO THE HONOUR AND COURAGE OF ALL
WHO SERVED IN THE ALLIED AIR FORCES

1939 – 1945

THEY SHALL GROW NOT OLD, AS WE THAT ARE LEFT GROW OLD:
AGE SHALL NOT WEARY THEM, NOR THE YEARS CONDEMN:
AT THE GOING DOWN OF THE SUN AND IN THE MORNING,
WE WILL REMEMBER THEM - PER ARDUA AD ASTRA

13 SEPTEMBER 1996

Canadian memorial, 1996.

Canadian memorial hangar to house 'Friday'.

material; and from the Museums, Libraries and Archives Council (as it now is) administered by the Science Museum and this was used to locate and fit World War Two-type lighting in the hangar.

I should mention here that some of the wartime buildings had been modified to suit the Americans when they dug-up the original three runways and replaced them with the current two-mile runway and forty acres of hard-standing. Not too many people realise that underneath this hard-standing the US air force built huge fuel storage tanks which were to be connected directly to a tanker stationed on the River Humber. The sub-station for these pipes still exists to the south-east of the airfield. It is general knowledge that after spending millions of dollars on the project, the USAF never did take over the airfield operationally.

CHAPTER 3 YAM Personalities

So many volunteers contributed to the creation of YAM but space does not permit me to list each and every one – but every bit of help was very much appreciated. However, a group who played a major role was the Air Gunners Association, led by Fred Stead. Apart from acting as stewards, they created the air gunners display. Each year former gunners from all over the UK visited the site and then took part in a memorial service. I was particularly thrilled at this part of the development of the museum because during my spell at the YARD I had witnessed the severe damage caused by enemy fighters who, in the early days of the war, always attacked the rear gunner to put him out of action. What I saw as a seventeen-year-old left an indelible impression. Once the air gunners' display had been opened, the team managed to secure examples of Fraser Nash and Boulton and Paul turrets, and after restoration the exhibition was in my opinion the best of its kind in the UK. Fred himself had served as a 'tail-end Charlie' on Halifaxes, dropping supplies into Belgium and Holland. Following his 'retirement' he devoted many hours into working at the museum.

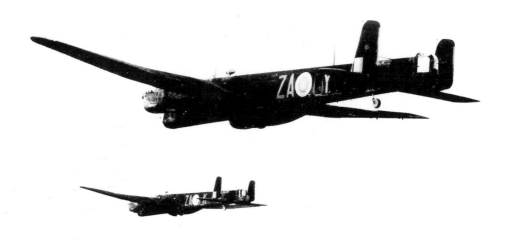

A 10 Squadron Whitley.

Another fascinating story developed concerning a husband and wife who visited YAM annually, their names I haven't recorded. Having greeted them on one particular visit, I asked the reason for their interest and it transpired that he had been a flight engineer serving with one of the Canadian squadrons flying Halifaxes in 6 Group. As the Canadians had never trained any flight engineers, each crew contained an RAF-trained flight engineer, and this particular visitor had been involved in a mid-air collision to the west of York when setting off on an operational sortie. He and his crew had baled out and their aeroplane had finally crashed near Goole. Having been fully loaded with bombs and fuel, there had been an almighty explosion. He went on to explain and show me a map identifying the place where each crew member had landed, between York and Goole. What had troubled him for so many post-war years was what had happened to the other Halifax they'd collided with. I assured him we would get one of our researchers to investigate the incident, and some months later I was able to report back to him that the other aeroplane involved had escaped serious damage and, having deposited its load of bombs in the North Sea, had returned to its Yorkshire 6 Group base. Another happy ending to a YAM story.

Yet another strange coincidence occurred when I was told a story (over a cup of coffee in the NAAFI) of a Whitley flying from a Yorkshire base into Germany dropping propaganda leaflets at the beginning of the war. They were instructed to land in France to refuel before returning to base. This particular crew who hadn't flown into the designated French airfield before, became somewhat lost and having seen a large grass field the pilot decided to set down in order to get his bearings. On a road alongside the grass field came a gentleman on a bicycle and the navigator jumped out of the Whitley to ask if he could point them in the right direction. But the cyclist wasn't French, he was German. As they were close to the French/German border, he knew the area and was able to tell them which way they should go. (Incidentally, my informant also told me that the German cyclist was later imprisoned for assisting the enemy.) I was telling this story to a visitor, again over a cup of coffee in the NAAFI, who let me finish and then said: "Well now, Mr. Robinson, I can confirm that the story is absolutely true, and when I get home I'll find the letter which my brother wrote to me recounting the incident and I'll send you a copy." The pilot was his brother. How is that for coincidence? The story must have caused a lot of amusement in the mess when they returned to squadron base.

Because of our facilities at Elvington, many of our veteran visitors were able to locate and re-connect with people they'd met whilst based in Yorkshire. None more so than the chairman of the Canadian branch of the museum, Doug Sample. Doug was based at East Moor operating as a mid-under gunner on Canadian Halifaxes. He must have paid one of the shortest visits to the UK when he completed a tour and was back in Canada in about six months. Doug's role was quite unusual, as not all the squadrons were equipped with aeroplanes with under-gun positions. The units were not happy when they were instructed to replace this gun position with the H2S radar blister. Although he was only here for six months, his heart never really left Yorkshire and he has been, without a doubt, one of the keenest supporters of the YAM.

The museum became a trust in 1985, and Rachel Semlyen was appointed chairman. Having already trained in public relations, she soon created an interest from the media. At the time I accepted the position of vice chairman and as I was still in full-time employment I could use some of the facilities of the company I managed, including transport and communication, and the occasional publication of a newsletter for circulation to members. This latter job was subsequently taken over by Norman Spence, who developed the theme and produced a very professional publication. I recall vividly how he would have to come to me and ask: could we afford to publish the next issue? Over the years, he has produced something like fifty editions and has done a superb job.

Sir Leonard Cheshire, Rachel Semlyen and Bobby Sage at YAM, 1987.

Other trustees from various professions, including the Royal Air Force and industry, volunteered their services, amongst them Robert 'Bobby' Sage and Dr. Mike Edwards whom I've already mentioned, Derek Reed of Pickerings bookshop in York (who specialised in aviation books) and Squadron Leader Ian Wormald, a standards instruction pilot.

In 1988 Rachel, who had been appointed to a full-time directorship of a local company, asked me if I would take over as executive chairman. My employers generously agreed to my early retirement and I was therefore able to accept Rachel's offer, with the approval of the other trustees. Little did I realise how much the whole enterprise would take over my life and at the same time provide me with fifteen years of immense pleasure and enjoyment, not least meeting hundreds of interesting people, many of them war veterans (and particularly those who had served in RAF squadrons).

After taking over on a virtually full-time basis, I soon realised that as the organisation was growing very rapidly and I had a forty-mile return journey each day to the museum, it was imperative that I should recruit three part-time managers. In the event, this turned out to be full-time on site managers with part-time pay. Jack Kilvington, a willing worker if ever there was one, took over general day-to-day affairs and was responsible for movements and security. Peter Slee became responsible for all exhibits, including archives, and Peter Dowthwaite took over as cashier. Each received a nominal amount which barely covered their expenses. Nevertheless, the system worked and for a total cost of about £12,000 per year I had successfully recruited an excellent staff along with Peter Minskip and Tony Arthur. Peter Slee, who was an apprentice trained woodworker, took on the responsibility of manufacturing hundreds of display cases and picture frames. He was also responsible for creating the replica French officers' mess which was officially opened with the Lord Mayor of York in attendance.

Uniform display at YAM by Peter Slee.

WAAF uniform display also by Peter Slee.

THE FRENCH CONNECTION

In June 1944, 77 Squadron moved lock stock and barrel to a nearby airfield, Full Sutton, where they were to be re-equipped with Halifax IIIs. In their place at Elvington arrived hundreds of Frenchmen who for a very short time used the 77 Squadron Halifaxes, until within a matter of weeks they were replaced by new Mk IIIs.

The effect on the locals must have been somewhat dramatic when their village was invaded by the French who, incidentally, wore an entirely different uniform from that of the RAF. Although I cannot be too specific I think these French airmen had been based in North Africa and had flown their aeroplanes there when the Germans over-ran their homeland. They were given the numbers 346 (Guyenne) and 347 (Tunisie) and were part of Bomber Command. When they first arrived at Elvington they had completed a conversion course onto Halifaxes at Lossiemouth in Scotland. I did hear some rather amusing stories about youngish RAF crews attempting to teach the French how to fly Halifaxes. Considering that the French aircrews were mature experienced fliers, one can imagine the *contre temps* arising. It must have been rather traumatic for these Frenchmen when some of their targets were in their own country, based on the D-Day landings which took place in June 1944.

One of YAM's original patrons was Air Chief Marshal Sir Gus Walker, who was at that time the base commander at RAF Pocklington, which controlled Elvington. It was the persuasive personality of Sir Gus which helped these two French squadrons to integrate into 4 Group.

Arrival of the French airmen at Elvington, 1944. 346 and 347 Squadrons.

French memorial at Elvington.

Sadly, the French losses were heavy and it must have been very difficult for them to fit into the local community. I remember meeting some of them in a pub in Piccadilly, York. Although there was no doubt that with extremely smart uniforms and broken English accents they were a great attraction to many of the local girls.

During March 1945, the Luftwaffe realised the damage they could do by following our bomber streams back to their bases, and one can imagine what an attractive target our airfields must have appeared when landing lights were lit-up. During one attempt to attack Elvington the pilot came in too low and hit a house on the York road just over a mile from the airfield, killing the crew and the occupants of the house. It has been claimed that this was the last German aeroplane to crash on British soil during the Second World War. Because of this attack flying control at Elvington instructed other returning French Halifaxes to find alternative airfields, and in one case an aircraft and its crew were lost having flown into the North York Moors.

After the end of hostilities, in October 1945 the British Government re-equipped both French squadrons with the new Halifax VI for them to return to their own country to form the post-war French air force. Apparently, the Frenchmen did several trips home with the bomb bays filled with many and varied domestic items, including bicycles. Tragically, one of the new Halifaxes crashed on take-off near Wheldrake, killing the crew and several passengers. A sad ending.

Each year, the French squadron association, known as Bombardier Lourds would hold a memorial service in Elvington village at their own impressive memorial stone. Naturally, when they heard of our plans for YAM they were anxious to get involved and their many contributions were invaluable. In particular, I recall the visits of General and Madame Calmel, who became such close friends and who opened the door, as it were, to the close co-operation which was to develop between the two organisations. The general and his wife were two of the nicest people you could wish to meet.

Another such member of Bombardier Lourds was Lt Col Louis Bourgaine, and I recall so clearly a special event which we organised when many of the French veterans were flown into Elvington, and we arranged with the RAF to fly-in several ex-members of 77 Squadron. On a glorious summers day we had crew buses with flying gear inside and after a quick change we were all very amused to see that nearly all the veterans had put on a bit of weight, 99% of the gear was rather on the small side! All the veterans were driven onto the site where we had the NAAFI van in situ distributing glasses of champagne, a truly enjoyable day and one which will stay in my memory always. Bombardier Lourds made many visits to England and we had some very happy social gatherings in the NAAFI when more than a fair amount of French wine was consumed.

Peter Slee worked very closely with Guy Jefferson, another volunteer stalwart, who built and brought onto the site some unique exhibits and one in particular attracted hundreds of visitors. Guy had researched every airfield in the UK and had produced a file which provided details of when and for what purpose each had been built, and the number of these, running into several thousands, fascinated the visitors. Many of them were ex-RAF and naturally they were delighted to read something about the bases they had served on. Guy also went on to produce a visual display showing over 1,000 crash sites in and around Yorkshire. Like his brother Bernard he is a truly talented historian. The third Jefferson brother, Lance, manufactured the cabinets with an equally professional appearance. We come to Bernard again on page 61.

Another stalwart who played such an important part in the early days was Sam Merrikin, an ex-Typhoon pilot, who took over the role of chief steward with the enormous responsibility of organising a team of volunteers to man the museum seven days a week. Without these volunteers YAM could not have operated.

Once we had become reasonably well established, there was a tremendous influx of World War Two uniforms, flying log books, medals, etc., and recording and storing these things was a huge problem. So many uniforms were donated to the museum, taking care of them became a bit of a headache, and the dear late Janet Voase took on this responsibility. I think that many former service personnel and relatives saw the museum, quite rightly, as an appropriate place to deposit their wartime 'bits and pieces'. But there were so many of them that at one time it became distressing and embarrassing having to tell people that we simply couldn't cope with any more. However, once the archive building had been developed a proper uniform store was established. I'm sure that this must be a problem in most collections – places like the RAF Museum and the Imperial War Museum must have thousands in store.

With all this building and development going on at YAM, I was still very much involved in continuing the Halifax project. Towards the end of World War Two both A.V. Roe and Handley Page were preparing designs for transport aeroplanes based on the wings of the Lancaster and the Halifax. In the case of the former, an aeroplane called the Tudor was developed, and in the case of Handley Page, a prototype Hermes was prepared for test flying in December 1945. Both of these types dispensed with the twin-fin tailplanes and the designers opted for single-fin and rudder. Sir Frederick Handley Page (always a competitor with A.V. Roe) was anxious to get the Hermes in the air before the Tudor, and the prototype Hermes with Jimmy Talbot at the controls took off from Radlett, tragically suffering elevator over-balance and killing the pilot and the flight engineer.

At the same time as producing the Hermes, a military version named the Hastings was successfully produced, and when it came to wings for our Halifax it occurred to me that if we could find and purchase some of these we'd be in business. Again, our friend Bill Hickey came to the rescue. He told me that a Hastings at RAF Catterick, no longer required for flying, was to be used for fire-fighting exercises and therefore the wings would not be required. Bill set up a meeting at Catterick for him, Bobby Sage and myself, to meet the commanding officer. We were shown the Hastings TG536, which had been used on the Berlin Airlift. It was explained to us that the only bit required for fire-fighting training was from the front spar forward of the fuselage, i.e. the object of the training exercise was to extricate the crew. I was told that I could buy wingtip to wingtip, which covered two outers, two intermediates, and the centre section containing both front and rear spars. As it turned out, the Ministry of Defence must have been feeling generous as I purchased all the wings for a nominal amount.

Next problem: who could we get to carry out the major task of a) dismantling the wings and b) transporting them to Elvington, as fuselage would obviously have to be removed from the wing sections. With yet another stroke of luck, in stepped another name to the story – Brian Berriman, who ran an engineering and haulage company, and they had lifting gear! Brian was used to assisting at road accidents where heavy vehicles were involved. A cheery, friendly and extremely hard-working individual, Brian offered to take on the whole project. For the first day's work at Catterick, Robert Sage and I were present when Brian decided that the quickest way to remove the fuselage sections was by cutting them with a welding torch, a procedure not normally associated with aeroplanes, and we had a tense moment when the station commander in his staff car, with flag flying, appeared on the scene just as Brian was lighting the torch. Here were two very different individuals – one from the military and the other a civilian, the latter used to getting things done in any way possible and quickly; they were on very different wavelengths. From a military point of view the aeroplane may have contained small amounts of 100 octane fuel, and the CO was obviously concerned about a premature fire. Fortunately, Robert stepped in and in a very diplomatic manner the problem was overcome. Brian's comment as the CO retreated was: "Who's that toffee-nosed bugger with the fancy 'at on?" But greater fun was yet to come.

"YAM was going to display a complete Halifax on a former Halifax base. The airframe would be as accessible as possible – a 'peoples' bomber'."

536

GPJ

Vitally important in the YAM Halifax was the Hastings lineage. Prime donor C.1A TG536 is illustrated during its heyday with 48 Squadron at Changi, Singapore, in 1960. MAP

Just what *is* YAM's 'Friday'?

A lot of people call the Elvington Halifax a **replica**. But much is new-build and other parts come from different types of aircraft. So, is it a **reconstruction** then? That doesn't fit the bill, either, implying that it is entirely new-build.

What we prefer is **re-creation** – this seems to convey the right message, a combination of skills and artefacts to bring about a Halifax by diverse means!

There is another term for YAM's *Friday the 13th* – **fabulous!**

get it. Thanks to locals, a friendly haulage company, the ferries and not least an RAF Boeing Chinook heavy

engines, undercarriage and tail surfaces and mating them to a new

1976. YAM determined that TG536 was in the best condition and had

By that date, the lads from Brough had extended their commitment

Reproduced from the December 2008 edition of Flypast *with permission from the publishers. Key Publishing Ltd. www.flypast.com*

After several visits, the five wing sections were separated and the front and rear fuselages were no longer attached. Having now prepared all the various sections for transporting to Elvington, Brian decided on the use of three articulated vehicles. When the wing sections were assembled the Hastings' wing span was well over 100 feet and the maximum chord width would be in the region of ten feet, therefore each vehicle would be classed as 'extra wide' and would therefore require police escort. Back at Elvington we had decided that the only place for the outer wings to be stored was in what is now called the main exhibition building and in order to gain access we had to knock the end gable completely out.

On the day of the intended move in the late 1980s, we had a 'heavy gang' of about twenty or thirty volunteers awaiting Brian and the convoy. Back at Catterick I was offering to help in any way I could, and sure enough Brian clearly defined my duty of the day. I had to proceed to the main entrance at Catterick airfield on the A1 southbound and chat-up the police so that they were 'on our side'. It later transpired that there was some doubt about the legality of the vehicles and the weight of their loads, and Brian wasn't too keen on the police investigating!

As it happened, the leading police car driver, when he realised that it was part of a Hastings we were moving, was more interested in the load than he was in the vehicle carrying it, as he had done some parachuting from one. What luck.

Many hours later the convoy arrived at the museum and with the tremendous energy and verve that Brian possessed the major task of unloading began. Because of the limited height, Brian was unable to get any sort of mechanical lifting gear into the building, and at one point he attached a block and tackle to the angle-iron which formed the roof trusses. Whilst he was operating this gear, he shouted to the rest of us to PUSH and at that very moment he damaged one of his fingers. There followed an outburst which included a considerable number of expletives, and in the silence that followed I introduced him to the Reverend Leonard Rivet, who was in 'civvies' and doing some of the pushing.

Having managed to place the outer wings

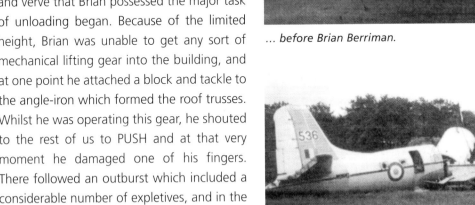

... before Brian Berriman.

... after Brian Berriman.

under cover, we housed the centre-section comprising the front and rear spars which passed through the fuselage and carried both inboard engines and undercarriage nacelles, in an old Nissen hut we had assembled temporarily on the perimeter track. The work then entailed removing the Hastings fuselage frames to return the assembly back to the Halifax configuration. The working conditions in the Nissen hut were poor, to say the least, and one of our enthusiastic members, Maurice Hepworth, who travelled a round trip of about forty miles each time he came to the museum, led the team carrying out the work. Maurice, who had been a flight engineer in the RAF with 640 Squadron, flying Halifaxes, became totally obsessed with the project. Virtually all his flying experience during the war was carrying out bombing operations over Germany and one could sympathise with his attitude as, like so many of our members, he was anxious to see a Halifax emerge from the ashes.

At about this time news came from Holland that the Royal Netherlands Air Force had located a crashed Halifax and intended excavating and retrieving parts where possible. This turned out to be a major undertaking as it entailed diverting streams and creating small dams. Maurice heard about this project and asked me if I had any objection to him going over there with a view to retrieving any parts which could possibly be useful for our Halifax. I did warn him that from my experience of crash sites I had seen during the war, where large aeroplanes

Hastings TG536 outer wings.

Hastings TG536, 1984.

had hit the ground at high speeds, there was usually very little left to salvage. In any case, in the fifty years since the end of the war, locals had already helped themselves to the metal parts, often for financial gain. Undeterred, Maurice went over to Holland at his own expense and phoned me daily, often with gruesome stories where human remains were being discovered. In any case, as I had forecast, no major units were dug out. I felt extremely sorry for him, as being ex-operational crew himself, he became emotionally involved in the whole event, and I was somewhat relieved when he returned to Elvington having spent four or five days in Holland.

A not dissimilar incident occurred a few years later when I received a phone call at my office in Leeds from the RAF based in Germany. It transpired that they had found some civilians digging out parts of a Halifax which had been shot down on 31st March 1944, during the infamous raid on Nuremberg. The officer in charge asked me if we would be interested in the four propeller hubs which, because of their shape and weight, had embedded themselves several feet into the ground. Naturally, I responded in the affirmative and then asked the obvious question: how do we get them to York? No problem, replied our RAF friend, we have transport which delivers to the north of England from time to time and we would be pleased to include these hubs on one of our trips. There was, however, one condition: could we research the details of the aeroplane and its crew, etc., so that he could pass the information to the authorities over there? This we duly did, and it turned out to be Halifax III LW687, from 432 Squadron

Assembling the tailplane (see pages 79-80).

59

"Yes it fits", chief technician N. Henshaw RAF.

RCAF 6 Group, based at East Moor, near York. I was delighted when the RAF delivered the four propeller hubs to our works in Leeds, and even more pleased when we started to dismantle them and found that the 'internals' which comprised hydraulic pistons, cams, etc., were all in near-perfect condition. As in the case of the Merlin engines, the oil had preserved these de Havilland airscrew hubs and needless to say they were fitted on to our aircraft. What was particularly pleasing was that the splines of the ex-Halifax hubs fitted perfectly on to the French-built Hercules prop-shafts when assembly took place in 1996.

Dear Maurice, who is no longer with us, also purchased for use at Elvington a video camera to record the work being carried out on the centre-section. One day, with a very satisfied smile on his face, he insisted I viewed the results of his camera work, but much to our amusement 90% of the unedited film recorded a lot of the ground and many women's and men's feet and legs. Maurice explained this by telling us he'd carried the camera around in his right hand, with it switched on. He is another character sadly missed at the museum.

CHAPTER 4 Restoration and the Halifax Project

GUN TURRETS

The whole picture was now becoming clearer, but there was still no sign of any gun turrets. Fortunately, however, I was contacted by an organisation called the Cotswold Aircraft Recovery Group who possessed a bedraggled but nonetheless genuine Boulton and Paul rear turret from a Halifax, which they agreed to let us have for restoration and eventual fitting to our aeroplane. When it arrived at Elvington it was in a sorry state, and quite frankly I had no idea what to do with it. Virtually all the Perspex which was specially moulded, had withered, broken or disappeared, and many of the 'mechanicals' were missing. Moreover, there were no Browning guns in it.

Someone who had grown up in Halifax country at Newton-on-Ouse, near Linton-on-Ouse and who was well-read on all things Halifax, was Bernard Jefferson. He had manufactured a superb model, not flyable, of a Halifax III with a wingspan of approximately six feet, and it was built into a flying display which he would exhibit at the squadron reunions, to much acclaim. Wonder of wonders and earning my eternal gratitude, Bernard volunteered to take on the restoration of the turret in his home-based workshop. My agreement with him was that we would supply any materials he required but there would be no cost for his labour. Of all the parts of the Halifax restoration programme, this reconstruction by Bernard must go down as little short of a miracle. Whilst I always knew what a brilliant and talented engineer he was, I could not have imagined in my wildest dreams what a remarkable result he would achieve. Despite having a full-time job, Bernard often worked five nights a week and each weekend on the project. His efforts must have totalled thousands of hours, but worth every minute.

A mid-upper turret was presented to us which had been used for many years as a garden cloche, and this was sent to Brough who fitted it into the fuselage section.

At this point in the Halifax story, I'd like to record that from the very beginning in 1983, I assured the trustees that I would not in any circumstances divert money which had been donated to the museum into the Halifax project. There had been some costs which had been borne by myself, but most of the work had been carried out by sponsorship. However, once our intentions regarding the Halifax became public knowledge, a lot of money was donated specifically for this project, and two members who played a big part in raising that money were

David Tappin and John Rayson, GAvA. I had first met John in the late 1940s when I went to work for Northern Motor Utilities Ltd, of which John's father was the general manager, but at that time I had no notion of his interest in the Halifax, nor did I know of his considerable ability as an artist. He used to tell me with some enthusiasm, how he and John Barry (the composer of many film soundtracks including *James Bond* films) used to cycle to Elvington during the war and watch the 77 Squadron Halifaxes taking off and landing. Once John found out about the existence of YAM he offered his services by producing the most evocative paintings of Halifaxes at various Yorkshire bases, and in one particular case during a visit by Sir Gus Walker, we had several hundred prints signed by the artist and Sir Gus. These raised considerable amounts of money for the Halifax project.

Brilliant restoration by Bernard Jefferson. Rear Boulton and Paul turret.

Aerial view of YAM.

We could now see the wings and the fuselage for the Halifax, but what about engines, front fuselage section, and undercarriage? I was not too concerned at this point about the internal fittings and felt that in my lifetime I'd be pleased to contribute to the creation of the external shape – and that future younger members could deal with the internal fitting out.

Once the Handley Page Building was complete, it provided an area to work in under somewhat better conditions than our hardy volunteers had encountered so far, and my next target was the front fuselage section from frames 1A to 16, which carried the crew quarters, except the air gunners' stations. Several years before my involvement with YAM I had visited Staverton airfield and had inspected the front fuselage section of a Halifax in a small museum there. This was Peter Thomas' pioneering Skyfame Aircraft Museum, which closed its doors in 1978. This nose is A.VII PN323, and it ultimately finished up at the Imperial War Museum in London. With nothing to lose and everything to gain, I wrote a begging letter to the curator explaining our progress on the Halifax at Elvington with a request: "Would they consider loaning their fuselage section to us?" I was informed by letter that in no circumstances could they agree to our request. By now, a lot of Halifax 'types' had heard about this situation and many of them wrote to the Imperial War Museum following up our request. After several weeks and many letters, the curator wrote to the last such correspondent saying that he'd heard more than enough about this subject and any further correspondence would simply go into the waste-paper basket!

MORE HELP FROM BROUGH

We then had no alternative but to start to manufacture our own front fuselage which was a most complex structure, containing the pilot's cockpit, flight engineer's position, wireless operator's and navigator's stations, etc. Fortunately we had the drawings, but where could we find a team of skilled airframe engineers to act as volunteers to carry out this mammoth task? One of our trustees, the late Dick Chandler, had worked as a test pilot at Blackburn and at British Aerospace. He had recently retired but taken on a voluntary job at Brough advising employees about to retire on how to fill their spare time with hobbies, etc. Dick, who was well known at Brough as 'Gentleman Jim' had the most pleasing of personalities and was extremely popular with the workforce.

After some discussion we agreed to invite a group of the retiring employees to visit us at Elvington. What an important move that proved to be. Already, Mike Edwards had 'allocated' Harry Woodford to assist us on anything aviation at Elvington. Harry was about to retire and from then on he and I worked closely together and he obtained our first propeller blade which we could reproduce by copying as we needed twelve of them. Fortunately, we had a mould manufactured from the blade which Harry obtained for us. A friend of mine, Peter Flanagan, produced it and again the gods were on our side when Ted Fawcett's son, Tim, persuaded his company to produce all twelve propeller blades – with a diameter of something like 13 feet each. I've already mentioned elsewhere that they were the wrong pitch, but as I've said several times to the critics – beggars can't be choosers.

Harry also obtained a Canberra T.4 WH 846 which was surplus at Preston and this was one of the first real aeroplanes we got on site, and from then on he also became very involved in working on the Halifax project.

Dick Chandler's team, lead by Ray Gadd, then arrived on site at Elvington. Ray and his colleagues (including John Hunt) were all apprentice trained and very highly skilled. I discussed with them what I had in mind, i.e. that we had all the detail drawings but to save a great deal of time and effort, we could make the frames (of which there were sixteen) from aircraft plywood, the originals were of course made from aluminium, but the rest of the fuselage would be manufactured as per the original DTD 390. Purists not involved in the project were critical of me for this decision, but as is so often the case with 'armchair critics', they themselves did not understand that in the absence of jigs and fixtures, it would have been well-nigh impossible to manufacture these frames in aluminium. In any case, the longerons, stringers and sheeting were all in the correct materials, and Ray had stressed the structure to make sure it was capable of withstanding a load of twelve people at any one time.

As a point of interest, the late Ray Gadd had broken his apprenticeship at Blackburn when he served on a Halifax squadron as an air gunner and had to ditch in the North Sea, and another member of the same crew was a well-known actor, the late Denholm Elliott. Ray told us the amusing story of how, when the aeroplane was floating in the sea, he and Denholm stood in the centre section waiting to escape through the top hatch and how they had deferred to each other – Ray saying "After you, Denholm", and Denholm replying with "No, after you,

Setting up the navigator's position.

Cockpit looking forward, showing the throttle box.

Very light pistol in flight engineer's position.

Gyro bomb site.

Ray". How typically English and how sadly we missed Ray, who played such a vital role in building Friday the 13th.

With the drawings available at Elvington, the team assembled, and work started on the huge task. The nucleus of the construction team included the two leaders, Ray Gadd and John

Hunt, Peter Brown, Bill Smith, Sid Taylor, Betty Hunt, Barrie Conway, Jim Willmott, Norman Gent, Brian Nottingham, Dave Waynes and L. Bates. It would be almost impossible these days to get together a similar team, not least because modern methods of manufacturing have introduced CNC (computer numerical control) to replace skilled men.

The average age of the team would have been something like seventy. The equipment available was minimal and in those days we had no health and safety at work personnel, we couldn't have afforded any anyway. Common sense had to prevail and I recall visiting the workshop several times a day to try to make sure 'the boys' didn't attempt anything too dangerous. What a marvellous crowd of blokes they were – and they all turned up as promised complete with tool boxes and clean overalls. My heartfelt thanks went out to every single one of them.

New frames and stringers fitted to the fuselage.

Front fuselage being checked to fit nose frames.

Pilot's cockpit structure being manufactured.

Peter Brown, Bill Smith, Sid Taylor, Betty Hunt, John Hunt, Barrie Conway, Jim Willmott, Norman Gent, Brian Nottingham, Dave Waynes and L. Bates.

Windscreen assembly fitted.

Engine nacelle.

Halifax being skinned, with window cut out after.

Pilot's instrument panel and throttle box before assembly.

Like most of the four-engined British-built bombers, the Halifax was constructed of nine major sub-assemblies and eventually at YAM our aircraft had to be assembled. None of the major components acquired by us in various ways had with it the thousands of nuts and bolts required to complete the aeroplane. Once again, luck was on our side and a local York concern, The Selby Nut and Bolt Company, came to our rescue and produced nuts and bolts in whatever shape and size we required, whether it be BA, BSF, or metric. And I recall vividly how, at the last minute, some of the volunteer workers would require items which were not standard, and the late Jack Kilvington made haste to the Selby company and at short notice they would produce whatever was required. They did a really magnificent job for us.

So many of our military aeroplanes specified and designed pre-war (some of them were flying within two years of conception) required considerable modification after initial test flights and this included problems with the airframe of the Halifax. Modifications, which ran into many thousands, were classified according to their urgency. For example, a class 1 modification meant that every aeroplane of the type had to be grounded until the work had been completed. I remember that in the 1943 period some of the squadrons were having occasional fatal accidents which were attributed incorrectly to 'rudder overbalance'.

Whilst we were fitting the rudders, I had a visit from two of my wartime friends, Lettice Curtis, an air transport auxiliary pilot, and Hedley 'Hazel' Hazelden, who became chief test pilot at Handley Page and with whom I flew on several occasions. During our informal discussions 'Hazel' made it abundantly clear that whilst so many people in post-war years referred to the problem as 'rudder overbalance', the truth of the matter was that the failing was fin stall. In other words, if the aeroplane was in a steep bank or if it side-slipped, the outboard fin stalled, due to the slab-side of the fuselage. This sometimes caused the aeroplane to go into a spin. I have long wanted to correct this misconception, and to explain why the Mk III and some of the Mk IIs and Vs were fitted with a square fin, which solved the problem. The Mk VI, fitted with Hercules 100 engines, could out-perform any other British-built four-engined bomber when it came to rate of climb, altitude, and straight and level speed, and several of the French visitors have told me that they would frequently go into raids in excess of 22,000 feet with the Mk VIs.

Included in the front fuselage team was John Hunt's wife, Betty, who spent many hours with a video camera recording the work in progress. In addition, and nothing to do with the Halifax project, the two Bettys (Betty Harris and Betty Hunt) supervised the sale of hundreds of bricks, which were intended for use in the T2 hangar. Many visitors who came to watch work in the Handley Page building were asked to sign a brick, perhaps to commemorate a loved one lost in World War Two, and thus, at £10 a time, contributed to the hangar fund. Another young worker in the team was the son of Group Captain Tom Eeles, who during his school holiday breaks volunteered to help us on the Halifax project. He is now an officer in the army air corps. It was nice to have a young man in the team. Working behind the scenes was the museum's president, Bobby Sage, who had a very comprehensive workshop at his home near Ripon, and he manufactured hundreds of small brackets for attaching the stringers to the front fuselage section.

The day eventually came when Ray Gadd and the team aligned the front fuselage for assembly to the rear of the aeroplane and as one would expect, it fitted like a glove. There were resounding cheers all round. It was so sad when Ray, who played such an important role in building the fuselage for the Halifax, died before the roll-out in 1996. Fortunately, John Hunt who had worked closely with Ray, took over the project and it was he who spent several years manufacturing and fitting out the 'internals'. A splendid job he did too, and his work was superbly covered in an article in the magazine *FlyPast* in December 2008.

MORE HELP FROM THE FRENCH

When the museum was under way, the French air force squadrons who had been based at Elvington formed an association called the Groupes Lourds and it was this group in France – no doubt with some prompting from Derek Reed who acted as our liaison officer with them, along with Ron Pontefract – who laid the foundation for the supply of four Bristol Hercules engines which the French had built under licence in the post-war years. In particular, the engines were used in the Nord Atlas transport, and much to our delight they offered us four such engines for our Halifax project. When Bobby Sage heard of this, he said once again: "When will your luck run out, Ian?"

And yet again the question was posed as to how we could get them to Elvington, each one weighing in the region of a ton? The French air force had the answer: they would fly them over. On 20th August 1987 a group of us watched as the C-160 Transall taxied up close to the museum site. We at YAM had no mobile lifting gear, but a kind gentleman from the village offered to bring along his fork-lift truck, which he also volunteered to operate. The young French crew, having disembarked, were talking to us whilst the lifting operation began, and I was talking to the pilot, who spoke very good English, and I asked him if the Transall was pressurised. Just as I spoke the last word there was a very loud bang when the forks on the fork-lift truck punched two holes in the fuselage. The young pilot, who remarkably had a grin on his face replied: "It was before we landed." A most embarrassing situation which the French skipper took so well, saying that they would fly back below 10,000 feet. Each engine was contained in a freshly prepared packing case, and our truly grateful thanks were conveyed to the Groupes Lourds and the French air force. Each member of the crew returned with a case of Sam Smith's beer to sign off a near perfect day.

Later on, we had to adapt the engine cowlings to the Halifax configuration, adding air scoops which were not relevant when used by the French. We were then advised by British Aerospace to remove items from the engines (which were not to be run anyway) in order to reduce the weight. BAe pointed out that the main spars onto which each engine had to be mounted were over forty years old and were severely corroded in parts. It would be several years before these engines could be fitted. Indeed, at this stage in the building of the Halifax, I found it extremely difficult to believe that what had started as a disused hen hut in the Outer Hebrides was at last beginning to take shape, and it was really looking as though we would achieve our ambition.

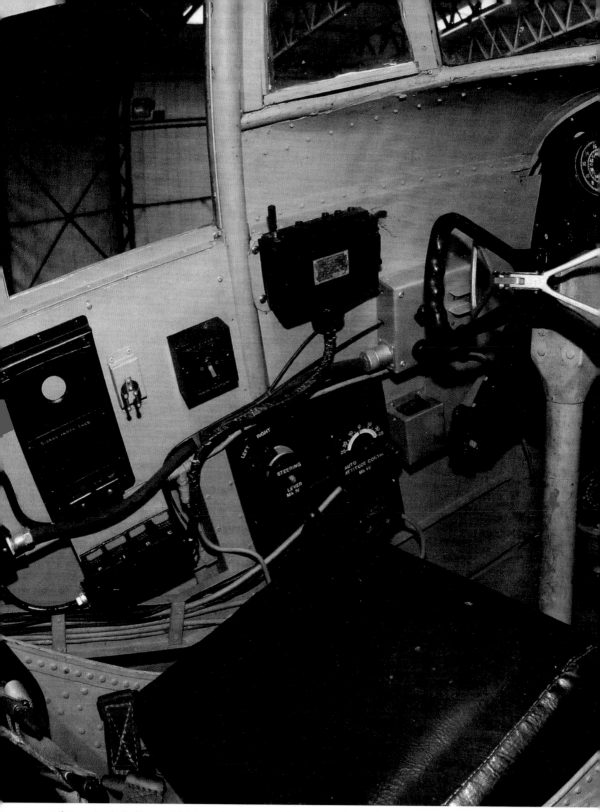

Pilot controls (left) and flight engine panel (right). Reproduced from the edition of FlyPast with permission from the publishers Key Publishing Ltd. www. Flypast.com. Sadly, Steve Fletcher, who took this photo, was killed soon after in an air crash.

How Friday the 13th was rebuilt piece by piece

Upper Turret
The top portion of the upper turret has been in use as a garden cloche in Derbyshire. Fittings, etc, came from a variety of sources. STEVE FLETCHER – WWW.AV8IMAGES.COM

Forward Fuselage
Built from scratch by YAM volunteers on site – illustrated in March 1995. KEN ELLIS

'Covered wagon'
This vital element came from a former Linton-on-Ouse Halifax and was salvaged for the project.

Main Image
To honour the two French units that flew Halifaxes from Elvington during the war, the starboard side of YAM'S re-creation is painted to represent Mk.VII NP763 'H7-N' of 346 'Guyenne' Squadron. The original is illustrated on a sortie out of Elvington in 1945. PETER GREEN COLLECTION

Propeller Hubs
Salvages from the wreck of MK.III LW687 of 432 Squadron RCAF – the aircraft went missing on a raid to Nurnberg on March 31, 1944. Propeller blades newly built by YAM volunteers. KEC

Centre Section and Inner Wings
Hastings C.1A TG536 languishing at the RAF Fire School, Catterick, Yorks, in 1976. This provided the all-important 'spine' to the airframe. MAP

Engines
Four Bristol Hercules 758 radials were flown into Elvington on board a French air force Transall C-160 airlifter on August 20, 1987. They came from two former French air force Nord Atlas transports (example illustrated at Biggin Hill in 1976). The engines were licence-built by SNECMA and arrived via Groupes Lourds – dedicated to the memory of French heavy bomber crews. KEC

Main Undercarriage
The massive undercarriage frame was manufactured by John Wilkinson of Pudsey, Yorks. The wheels and tyres are 'stock' Halifax items. STEVE FLETCHER – WWW.AV8IMAGES.COM

Outer Wings
The outer wings were unused, 'stock' items. They were found, including their wonderful transit case, in a scrapyard in the south of England and are pictured arriving in Elvington. YAM

Rear Fuselage
Built from new by BAe apprentices at Brough, Humberside. Illustrated is the former Isle of Lewis hen hut mated up to the BAe-built rear fuselage and rear turret at Elvington, May 1989. KEC

Tailplane
Based upon a section salvaged from the wreck of Mk.V LL505 of 1659 Conversion Unit which crashed near Coniston in the Lake District on October 22, 1944. Remainder built from new by YAM volunteers

Rear Turret
Basic frame for the Boulton Paul turret came from the Cotswold Aircraft Restoration Group. Brothers Bernard and Guy Jefferson carried out the restoration in York

Tail Wheel
Salvaged in France. This came from the wreck of Mk.III HX271 of 466 Squadron RAAF which was shot down on a raid to Trappes on June 3, 1944.

Tail Fins and Rudders
Tail fins built from new by BAe apprentices at Brough, Humberside; rudders also newly created by YAM volunteers. STEVE FLETCHER – WWW.AV8IMAGES.COM

'Hen Hut'
The 'founder member', the mid-fuselage section that had served as a hen hut on the Isle of Lewis. Illustrated in situ in May 1979. KEC

Another person who was of tremendous help to me throughout this time was an ex-Halifax flyer, Victor Bingham. He and I had got together when he started to write the book *Halifax Second to None* which was published in 1986. Victor, like myself, had always felt that the Halifax had suffered bad publicity in the post-war years (a Lancaster/Halifax situation rather like the Spitfire/Hurricane one had developed), and it was Victor's intention in writing the book to try historically to correct the bad press. He and I exchanged many views on the subject, and I remember telling him of some of the remarks I'd heard

French air force C-160 Transall lands at Elvington with donated engines.

from the Canadians of 6 Group who flew their Mk IIIs from Yorkshire bases.

One pilot with whom I became particularly friendly was Squadron Leader Wib Pierce. He and his English flight engineer, the late Fred Haynes, were quite emphatic about how much they preferred the Halifax for operational flying and were far from happy when they had to transfer to the Lancaster. Wib's comments were: "It was like changing from a Cadillac [Halifax] to a Ford [Lancaster]." They claimed that the Halifax III was faster, with a better rate of climb and had a much stronger airframe, but conceded that it could not carry the bomb load of the Lancaster. A further point not widely known is that a university student researched the success of crews baling out of damaged aeroplanes, and found that the higher rate of success was from the Halifax.

C-160 Transall unloading Bristol Hercules engines at Evington.

AN "LUCKY" THOMSON
427 SQDN. – LEEMING.

Ian 'Lucky' Thompson. 427 Squadron, waiting for the 'Lancs' to catch up!

THE THREE LONDONERS

Once we had started looking in detail at the outer wings from the Hastings at Catterick, we were to discover very badly corroded sections of the main spars, and this caused us considerable worry. But yet again, good fortune was shining down on us as in London we had three very loyal supporters, all ex-RAF. They were Bill Lord, Don Smith and Alf Belson. They were all very active in the local RAF Association, and much to my amazement Bill phoned one day to say they had discovered two brand new Hastings outer wings at a scrap dealer's yard in the south of England. They were in box packing cases and to all intents and purposes they were brand new. Apparently the 'scrappie' had bought them purely for the wood content – as you can imagine the packing cases were pretty big.

Our three supporters set about raising several thousand pounds to purchase the wings on our behalf and to pay for transporting them to Elvington. A truly magnificent effort from these exceptionally great supporters. The 'three Londoners' as we nicknamed them, continued to support the museum by raising money (I think the Chiswick branch of RAFA became involved) and Bill and Don collected some undercarriage wheels for us. Bill's part-time job was working for television, chauffeuring various celebrities about, but his own mode of transport was a Morris 1000 estate, complete with trailer, and his mate Don told me of frequent hair-raising adventures when they were collecting bits and pieces for the Halifax project.

The pièce de resistance was when Bill wanted to apply heat to an axle that was locked in a Halifax wheel hub. He had a friend who worked in the Concorde hangar at Heathrow and without any hesitation he took the offending hub into the hangar where they were working on Concorde. Bill lit his welding torch and just before he started to work on our bit, security men appeared from all directions. Bill, Don, Morris 1000, trailer and all were evicted unceremoniously and told: "Don't ever come here again!" Bill took all this in his stride, but Don was a little disturbed to say the least.

Our next major problem was the undercarriage. With the exception of the Halifax V, all were equipped with the French-designed Messier units, comprising a large casting in magnesium. To the best of my knowledge at that time no examples existed, and because it was not designed by Handley Page, no drawings were available to us. However, much to my surprise and delight, I was told that one example of the main wheel arch did indeed exist and it was owned by the RAF Museum, although in store at Cardington in Bedfordshire. New to our scene was an engineer called John Wilkinson, who ran his own engineering works near Leeds. John said that if we could get this example of an undercarriage leg, he could use it as a pattern to manufacture the rest from scratch. Jack Kilvington drove down to Cardington and in what used to be the original airship hangars found our much-wanted undercarriage leg. Jack was very impressed by these huge hangars containing hundreds of parts from historic aeroplanes, including World War Two engines. The RAF Museum kindly loaned us this casting for us to use as a pattern. This was duly transferred to John's works where manufacturing began, and he would invite me over from time to time to see work in progress.

Unused Hastings outerwing, 1989.

Finally, the newly-produced items were delivered to Elvington and caused tremendous admiration for the fine work that John had completed. Then came a very embarrassing bit – John asked me where he should send the invoice! This took me aback not a little, as I had assumed that the work was being done free of charge. When I explained this to him, being the gentleman he was, he made fun of the incident and no money changed hands. The story has a sad

Don Smith, Alf Belson and Bill Lord.

ending though as John then put his business up for sale and told me he'd like to come and work with us on the Halifax project for at least three days a week. But it was not to be, for having completed the sale of his company, he was stricken with cancer and died within a few weeks. John's wife asked us to place a seat on the site in his memory; which is a tribute to a fine gentleman and good friend. Sadly, he never saw the Halifax assembled.

Two major volunteers: John Hunt and Neil
Henshaw.

Restored undercarriage, with John Wilkinson
(right).

Restored undercarriage leg by John Wilkinson.

THE TAILPLANE

In the early 1990s the one major component which did not figure in our planning was the tailplane assembly, and with our target completion date looming, Harry Woodford, Phil Kemp and Peter Minskip and I took on the responsibility of producing same, although it was something of a temporary measure. Unfortunately, the final sub-assembly was built with anhedral of $2\frac{1}{2}°$ port and starboard, instead of $1\frac{1}{2}°$. My friend John Hunt assured me that at a later date they would put things right, but at least our work allowed us to keep to our target date.

Once the Halifax became mobile, but without wings, we had another official naming day in spring 1994, when the two station commanders from Linton-on-Ouse and Leeming, named the Halifax Friday the 13th and that day was enjoyed by several hundred people with a fly-past of Jet Provosts and Tornados.

Rear bay tailplane not fitted.

Rudder part complete.

Jig for leading edge tailplane.

Fitting elevator hinge bolts.

Skinning the tailplane.

Tailplane before skinning.

Fin attachment to the tailplane.

CHAPTER 5
Friday the 13th

WHY FRIDAY THE 13TH?

When it came to selecting a name for our Halifax I discussed this at length with Bobby Sage and several possibilities came to mind – the name of a 77 Squadron Halifax, one from the French 346 or 347 Squadron, or Cyril Barton VC's aeroplane. I was anxious to draw public attention to our project and as Friday the 13th had become well-known during and after the war, as one of the most remarkable bomber aircraft, we thought it most appropriate.

In February 1944 I had been sent to Handley Page airfield at Radlett on a course of both ground and flying training. Whilst I was there a batch of new Halifax IIIs of the LV series were coming off the production line. My log book records that I flew LV939 to 948 as flight engineer with chief test pilot Jimmy Talbot and production test pilot 'Sandy' Sanders. It is fairly certain that LV907 (later to become Friday) was produced at about that time and I may well have done some ground engineering work on it.

LV907 was flown from Radlett by an air transport auxiliary pilot to an RAF maintenance unit where it would be fitted with additional equipment such as radar. It was then flown to Leconfield in Yorkshire, an airfield in 4 Group, RAF Bomber Command. Two Halifax squadrons, 466 and 640, already existed at Leconfield. LV907 was flown to nearby Lissett, home of 158 Squadron (also in 4 Group) where it was given the squadron code letters NP and the letter F, an individual identification.

(Many numbers and letters have confused historians because it was not uncommon to use the same identification letter on more than one aeroplane, for example if A for Apple went missing or was transferred, its replacement also became A for Apple. At the works and at YARD we used only serial numbers. There is one instance where a Halifax is listed as shot down/destroyed on the Nuremberg raid in March 1944, but it was flown at York several months later and is recorded in my log book.)

This infamous raid was also one of LV 907's first sorties. This event, which went so badly wrong, was researched and written about by Martin Middlebrook. Heavy losses were suffered, but 158 Squadron's LV 907 survived. One aircraft which did not return to base was LW 687 of 432 Squadron Royal Canadian Air Force based at East Moor and which was later to be the source of the four hubs for our project at Elvington.

Wings for Victory, raising money in Liverpool.

OPERATIONS LOG – 'FRIDAY THE 13TH'

NO	DATE	TARGET	PILOT	OUT	IN
1	MAR 30/31 1944	NUREMBURG	F/SGT J HITCHMAN	22:03	05:34
2	APR 9/10 1944	VILLENEUVE ST GEORGE MY	P/O C E SMITH	20:40	02:05
3	APR 10/11 1944	TERGNIER MY	P/O C E SMITH	20:40	01:47
4	APR 18/19 1944	TERGNIER MY	P/O C E SMITH	20:55	01:32
5	APR 20/21 1944	OTTIGNIES MY	P/O C E SMITH	21:05	01:00
6	APR 22/23 1944	DUSSELDORF	P/O C E SMITH	22:27	03:17
7	APR 24/25 1944	KARLSRUHE	P/O C E SMITH	21:33	03:57
8	APR 26/27 1944	VILLENEUVE ST GEORGE MY	P/O C E SMITH	21:35	02:41
9	APR 28 1944	AULNOYE MY	P/O C E SMITH	00:49	04:45
10	APR 30/MAY 1 1944	ACHERES MY	P/O C E SMITH	21:33	01:49
11	MAY 1/2 1944	MALINES MY	F/SGT J HITCHMAN	21:50	01:40
12	MAY 9, 1944	MORSALLINES	P/O C E SMITH	00:49	04:23
13	MAY 10/11 1944	LENS MY	F/SGT EVANS	21:24	01:08
14	MAY 11/12 1944	COLLINE BEAUMONT	P/O C E SMITH	23:03	02:25
15	MAY 12/13 1944	HASSELT MY	P/O C E SMITH	21:57	02:17
16	MAY 19/20 1944	BOULOGNE MY	P/O C E SMITH	23:05	03:05
17	MAY 24/25 1944	AACHEN EAST MY	P/O C E SMITH	22:48	02:52
18	MAY 27/28 1944	BOURG LEOPOLD TANK	P/O C E SMITH	23:45	04:28
19	JUN 1/2 1944	FERME D'URVILLE RS	P/O C E SMITH	22:49	03:20
20	JUN 2/3 1944	TRAPPES MY	P/O C E SMITH	22:17	03:31
21	JUN 6, 1944	MAISY CG	P/O C E SMITH	00:50	05:29
22	JUN 6/7 1944	CHATEAUDUN MY	P/O C E SMITH	23:34	05:06
23	JUN 8 1944	VERSAILLES MY	P/O C E SMITH	00:09	04:33
24	JUN 10 1944	LAVAL AF	P/O C E SMITH	00:15	05:21
25	JUN 12/13 1944	AMIENS MY	P/O C E SMITH	23:07	03:13
26	JUN 16/17 1944	STERKRADE OR	F/SGT R J CHILCOTT	23:09	03:36
27	JUN 17/18 1944	ST MARTIN L'HORTIER V-1	F/SGT R J CHILCOTT	22:56	03:06
28	JUN 22 1944	SIRACOURT V-1	F/O R E NEW	13:30	17:33
29	JUN 23/24 1944	OISEMONT NEUVILLE AU BOIS V-1	F/SGT E PAULSEN	22:50	02:38
30	JUN 25 1944	LE GRAND ROSSIGNOL V-1	F/SGT R J CHILCOTT	01:14	05:21
31	JUN 27 1944	MARQUISE/MIMOYECQUES V-3	F/SGT R J CHILCOTT	11:40	15:15
32	JUN 28 1944	WIZERNES V-1	W/O L FULKER	05:21	08:43

OPERATIONS LOG – 'FRIDAY THE 13TH'

NO	DATE	TARGET	PILOT	OUT	IN
33	JUN 30 1944	VILLERS BOCAGE TANK	F/SGT R J CHILCOTT	17:58	21:51
34	JUL 1 1944	OISEMONT NEUVILLE AU BOIS V–	P/O C E SMITH	15:29	19:07
35	JUL 7 1944	CAEN	F/O G H MONTGOMERY	19:31	23:44
36	JUL 12/13 1944	FERME DU FORRESTEL V–1	P/O C E SMITH	23:36	03:27
37	JUL 18 1944	CAEN	P/O C E SMITH	03:21	07:23
38	JUL 20/21 1944	BOTTROP OR	P/O C E SMITH	23:30	03:15
39	JUL 23/24 1944	LES CATELLIER V–1	F/SGT D A WATERMAN	22:20	02:24
40	JUL 24/25 1944	STUTTGART	P/O C E SMITH	21:22	05:34
41	JUL 25/26 1944	WANNE EICKEL OR	P/O L FULKER	22:39	03:27
42	JUL 28 1944	FORET DE NIEPPE V–1 DEPOT	P/O C E SMITH	16:03	19:39
43	JUL 29 1944	FORET DE NIEPPE V–1 DEPOT	F/SGT D A WATERMAN	17:36	21:47
44	AUG 1 1944	CHAPELLE NOTRE DAME (AB)	P/O C E SMITH	19:45	22:43
45	AUG 2, 1944	L'HEY V–1	F/SGT D A WATERMAN	18:32	22:24
46	AUG 3 1944	FORET DE NIEPPE V–1	F/SGT D A WATERMAN	18:12	21:23
47	AUG 5 1944	FORET DE NIEPPE V–1	F/SGT D A WATERMAN	11:13	14:40
48	AUG 6 1944	FORET DE NIEPPE V–1	F/SGT D A WATERMAN	11:05	14:29
49	AUG 7/8 1944	TOTALISER THREE (NORMANDY)	F/SGT D A WATERMAN	20:41	00:31
50	AUG 9 1944	BOIS DE LA HAIE V–1	F/SGT D A WATERMAN	11:15	15:02
51	AUG 11 1944	FERFAY V–1	F/SGT D A WATERMAN	17:37	21:30
52	AUG 12/13 1944	BRUNSWICK	F/SGT D A WATERMAN	21:18	02:58
53	AUG 14, 1944	TRACTABLE 21A (NORMANDY)	F/SGT D A WATERMAN	11:47	15:55
54	AUG 15 1944	EINDHOVEN AF	F/SGT D A WATERMAN	09:46	13:36
55	AUG 16/17 1944	KIEL	F/SGT D A WATERMAN	21:42	02:21
56	AUG 18/19 1944	STERKRADE OR	F/SGT D A WATERMAN	22:19	03:01
57	24 AUG 44	BREST SHIPPING	F/O D W MCADAM	09:53	14:54
58	AUG 25/26 1944	BREST – POINTE DES ESPAGNOLS	F/SGT A W MEADEN	20:52	02:24
59	AUG 27 1944	HOMBERG HEERBECK OR	F/SGT H J HARMER	11:40	16:02
60	AUG 31 1944	LA POURCHINTE (AB)	F/SGT A W MEADEN	12:38	16:11
61	SEP 3 1944	SOESTERBERG AF	F/SGT H J HARMER	15:55	19:03
62	SEP 9 1944	LE HAVRE (AB)	P/O A W MEADEN	06:42	10:40
63	SEP 10 1944	LE HAVRE GARRISON	P/O D A WATERMAN	15:05	18:25
64	SEP 11 1944	LE HAVRE (AB)	F/O S E REES	05:10	10:04

OPERATIONS LOG – 'FRIDAY THE 13TH'

NO	DATE	TARGET	PILOT	OUT	IN
65	SEP 12 1944	GELSENKIRCHEN – BUER OR	P/O D A WATERMAN	10:59	15:26
66	SEP 13 1944	GELSENKIRCHEN – NORDSTERN OR	P/O D A WATERMAN	15:57	20:38
67	SEP 15/16 1944	KIEL	P/O D A WATERMAN	22:20	03:47
68	SEP 17 1944	BOULOGNE	P/O D A WATERMAN	07:10	10:26
69	SEP 23 1944	NEUSS (AB)	P/O D A WATERMAN	18:54	21:57
70	SEP 25 1944	CALAIS (AB)	S/LDR A G SLATER	08:21	12:18
71	SEP 26 1944	CALAIS GARRISON	P/O D A WATERMAN	09:35	13:24
72	OCT 6 1944	STERKRADE OR	F/O D A WATERMAN	14:28	18:57
73	OCT 7 1944	KLEVE	F/O D A WATERMAN	12:00	15:45
74	OCT 9 1944	BOCHUM	F/O N TILSTON	17:21	23:03
75	OCT 14 1944	DUISBURG	F/O D A WATERMAN	06:26	11:51
76	OCT 15 1944	DUISBURG	F/O D A WATERMAN	00:18	06:14
77	OCT 15 1944	WILHELMSHAVEN	F/SGT H J HARMER	17:57	21:30
78	OCT 21 1944	HANNOVER	F/O T H SINCLAIR	16:34	18:03
79	OCT 23 1944	ESSEN	F/SGT H J HARMER	16:28	21:45
80	OCT 25 1944	ESSEN	F/O N G GORDON	12:29	17:31
81	OCT 28 1944	DOMBERG CG	F/O D A WATERMAN	09:35	12:32
82	OCT 29 1944	ZOUTLANDE	F/O N G GORDON	10:14	13:45
83	NOV 29 1944	ESSEN	F/O N G GORDON	02:24	08:13
84	NOV 30 1944	DUISBURG	SGT R KAYE	16:29	22:14
85	DEC 2/3 1944	HAGEN	F/O F M COMPTON	17:55	00:17
86	DEC 5/6 1944	SOEST	F/O D H ROBINSON	18:02	00:32
87	DEC 6 1944	OSNABRUCK (AB)	F/O D H ROBINSON	15:53	17:26
88	DEC 12 1944	ESSEN	F/O D H ROBINSON	16:20	20:17
89	DEC 18 1944	DUISBURG	F/O D H ROBINSON	02:51	09:14
90	DEC 21 1944	COLOGNE	F/O N G GORDON	15:05	21:13
91	DEC 24 1944	ESSEN – MULHEIM (AB)	F/O D H ROBINSON	11:33	15:19
92	DEC 26 1944	ST VITH AS	F/O D H ROBINSON	12:56	17:23
93	DEC 28 1944	OPLADEN	F/O N G GORDON	03:09	08:56
94	DEC 30/31 1944	COLOGNE	F/O N G GORDON	17:16	00:04
95	JAN 1 1945	DORTMUND CP	F/O D H ROBINSON	16:49	21:24
96	JAN 2 1945	LUDWIGSCHAFEN CW	F/O N G GORDON	15:00	21:55

NO	DATE	TARGET	PILOT	OUT	IN
97	JAN 5 1945	HANOVER	F/O N G GORDON	16:49	22:02
98	JAN 14 1945	SAARBRUCKEN MY	P/O N TILSTON	10:42	17:32
99	JAN 16/17 1945	MAGDEBURG	F/LT N G GORDON	18:46	00:38
100	JAN 22/23 1945	GELSENKIRCHEN	F/LT N G GORDON	18:48	00:32
101	FEB 1 1945	MAINZ TC	F/LT N G GORDON	16:21	22:49
102	FEB 4 1945	GELSENKIRCHEN	F/LT N G GORDON	17:05	22:48
103	FEB 7/8 1945	GOCH AS	F/LT N G GORDON	19:02	00:41
104	FEB 9 1945	WANNE EICKEL OR	F/LT N G GORDON	03:18	08:53
105	FEB 13/14 1945	BOHLEN SYN OR	F/LT N G GORDON	18:39	02:27
106	FEB 14/15 1945	CHEMNITZ RED AS	F/LT N G GORDON	17:04	00:57
107	20/21 FEB 45	REISHOLZ	S/LDR A G SALTER	21:43	04:15
108	FEB 21 1945	WORMS RRC	F/SGT R KAYE	17:16	23:41
109	FEB 23 1945	ESSEN	F/SGT R KAYE	11:57	17:46
110	FEB 24 1945	KAMEN OR	S/LDR A G SALTER	12:44	19:08
111	FEB 27 1945	MAINZ	S/LDR A G SALTER	12:41	19:34
112	MAR 2 1945	COLOGNE TC	F/O A W A ELLEY	07:02	12:39
113	MAR 3/4 1945	KAMEN TC	F/LT N G GORDON	18:15	00:30
114	MAR 5/6 1945	CHEMNITZ (PORT OUTER U/S)	F/LT N G GORDON	17:14	01:45
115	MAR 11 1945	ESSEN	F/LT N G GORDON	11:44	17:08
116	MAR 12 1945	DORTMUND MY	F/LT N G GORDON	13:07	19:10
117	MAR 13 1945	WUPPERTAL	F/LT N G GORDON	12:30	18:10
118	MAR 14 1945	HOMBERG AS	F/LT N G GORDON	17:03	23:11
119	MAR 15 1945	HAGEN TC	F/LT N G GORDON	17:04	23:15
120	MAR 19 1945	WITTEN TANK	F/LT N G GORDON	00:27	07:15
121	MAR 20 1945	RECKLINGHAUSEN	F/LT N G GORDON	10:06	15:27
122	MAR 21 1945	RHEINE	F/LT N G GORDON	14:56	19:43
123	MAR 24 1945	GLADBECK	F/O H WHEELER	09:03	15:09
124	MAR 25 1945	MUNSTER MY	F/O H WHEELER	07:23	12:37
125	APR 4/5 1945	HARBURG RHENANIA OR	F/O H WHEELER	20:02	01:34
126	APR 8/9 1945	HAMBURG UBW	F/O H WHEELER	19:33	01:47
127	1 APR 18 1945	HELIGOLAND CG	F/SGT W DARGAVEL	11:18	15:16
128	APR 25 1945	WANGEROOGE CG	F/O H WHEELER	14:47	18:45

Brian Gaunt (artist) reproduces nose artwork.

It was shortly after the Nuremberg raid that LV 907 was 'christened' Friday the 13th by its crew in March 1944. By October of that year, it had done eighty ops. After a month's break, for major servicing, LV907 resumed operations and the 100th was to Gelsenkirchen on 22nd January 1945. After, Flight Lieutenant Gordon, the pilot, paid this tribute: "We always feel absolutely confident in her. She flies right and she always gets there." LV907's last op was to Wangerooge on 25th April 1945, when 4 Group aircraft carried out their last attack on an enemy target. This brought 907's final total to 128 ops.

Unfortunately I have no idea who decided on the name. However Jack Weeks MBE was the artist who wielded the paint brush and our artwork was carried out by the very talented Brian Gaunt.

Friday the 13th is much detailed in an article in *Aviation News* published in October 1992 and written by Bill Chorley. His excellent research paints a fascinating picture of the many difficult sorties Friday carried out and just how many different crews used it: Canadian, New Zealand, Australian, and, of course RAF personnel.

Since our YAM Halifax started its life when HR792 crashed near Stornoway in 1945 and that the road to the stage reached at Elvington in 1996 had been a long and rugged one, it is quite appropriate that our Halifax should carry the same proud name as one of its outstanding

Nose art on the original Friday the 13th, on display in Oxford Street, London 1945.

predecessors. One which kept going in spite of everything put in its way, through thick and thin, right to the end of the war.

In the summer of 1945 after the end of hostilities, Friday the 13th together with several other aeroplanes went on show on a bomb site in London's Oxford Street, and attracted great attention from the public. Sadly, it was then, along with several hundred other Halifaxes, for example Wings for Victory on pages 82-83, on show to raise money in Liverpool, despatched to YARD at Clifton airfield where we, I am ashamed to admit, then scrapped all of them to be turned into pots and pans.

MORE AEROPLANES ACQUIRED

To return to the development of the museum, one of our trustees was a retired Air Vice-Marshal, Harry Southgate, and it was through his good offices that we were able to purchase an English Electric Lightning which, in the 1980s, was the fastest jet in use by the RAF. (Halifaxes were also manufactured by English Electric alongside Handley Page, at their Lancashire site, with over 2,000 bombers being built at the factory during World War Two.) Fortunately, I came across a gentleman who worked for BAe at Warton in Lancashire, and who had a most unusual wish to own a Lightning as he had seen the development of this aeroplane during his working life at BAe. He offered to put up the money to purchase one of the type on his behalf, and through Harry Southgate the wheels were set in motion.

Towards the end of negotiations things happened very quickly and on one particular day I was asked to place a bankers order for the required amount with the Ministry of Defence in

Mk II Halifaxes at the English Electric factory, Preston.

Harrogate – and to do it rather quickly. We did not of course have that sort of money at the museum, nor did I have enough in my personal account. I went along to see my bank manager and asked for an order for several thousand pounds. "What do you want the money for?" he asked me. "To purchase a jet fighter," I replied. "No, seriously, why do you want the money?" To cut a long story short, I deposited the required finance with the Ministry of Defence the following day and I was delighted to report to the trustees that the RAF would be flying in a Lightning two days later. Naturally, we had a reception party awaiting its arrival at Elvington, where it did a spectacular, very fast low pass over the museum. The aeroplane was Peter Chambers' Lightning F.6 XS 903 and it flew in on 18th May 1988 flown by Wing Commander Jake Jarron.

Another aeroplane which we obtained for several thousand pounds, with the help of 609 Squadron Association, was a mock-up Spitfire to be used as a gate-guardian, and which cost several thousand pounds. The association suggested that if we could pay half, then the ownership of the aeroplane would be YAM's. This was a very successful exercise which cost the museum in the region of £3,000.

A few years later in November 1993, I was approached by aircraft enthusiast, Andre Tempest's father, who said he was quite prepared to purchase another fly in aeroplane but

Friday 13th and Lusty Linda – two generations of aircraft juxtaposed.

could I negotiate on his behalf? At this particular time the Handley Page Victor was being taken out of service, and I was very lucky to get hold of Lusty Linda, which had been used to refuel the Vulcan during the Falklands campaign. Having completed the deal, we were informed that the Victor would be flown in a few days later and once again we had a reception party waiting on the airfield. A good friend at that time was the station commander at RAF Linton-on-Ouse, Group Captain Tom Eeles, and on the day of the Victor's arrival he very kindly escorted it in flying a Jet Provost – another milestone in the history of the Yorkshire Air Museum.

Based at RAF Leeming was a Meteor twin-jet NF.14 WS788 destined for YAM, and a chief technician by the name of Neil Henshaw was permitted to work on restoring the aeroplane in his own time (at Leeming). An amusing incident occurred there when the minister of defence was paying an official visit and was intrigued to see this rather old Meteor amongst the shiny new Tornados. The minister approached Neil and asked: "What exactly is this project?" Quick-thinking Neil replied: "Sir, this is our secret weapon in the cold war." The minister walked away with a smile on his face and nothing more was said.

Chief technician Henshaw ultimately became one of our own 'secret weapons'. After being posted to Brize Norton in Oxfordshire, he continued making parts for the Halifax in his own time. Then on a special day at the museum, Neil arrived with his father, an ex-Halifax flier, and invited me to present to his father the medals he'd earned during the war but which he had never collected. This was a very special day but also a very emotional one. Neil subsequently negotiated on our behalf for two brand new undercarriage wheels on which Friday the 13th currently stands. Neil was to figure greatly when the time came to assemble all the major parts of the Halifax, an event which took place in July 1996.

As we had on site a lot of heavy lifting equipment, quite a large crowd had gathered to witness this historic event. This involved fitting four engines, four airscrews, and undercarriage legs – it was a day we'd all been looking forward to. And as in any organisation which is basically run by volunteers, many of the onlookers behaved as if they were experts, and it became obvious to me that whilst the photographer was telling us how to put the engines in, tempers were getting a bit frayed and accidents might well happen. I had previously contacted Neil's commanding officer and obtained special permission for him to be with us for this major event. After much superfluous advice from many of the onlookers, Neil stood on top of the aeroplane, about 12 feet off the ground, and made it quite clear that he was in charge, and in no uncertain manner he invited the 'experts' to stay by all means – but to keep their bloody mouths shut! This instruction worked a treat and from then on everything went like clockwork and according to plan. Neil was to gain the commanding officer's commendation for his work on the Halifax.

Another aeroplane which was a great attraction at the museum was a private venture undertaken by Tony Agar, who had spent almost a lifetime in constructing a complete Mosquito. Totally dedicated to this project, Tony had sought parts virtually on a world-wide scale, even including special plywood from Canada. When he first started work at Elvington, I had arranged for Brian Berriman to transport major pieces of the Mosquito which Tony had stored in and around his private house. To start with, the facilities we were able to provide were far from perfect. On one particularly distressing occasion the Nissen hut we had provided

Work in progress 1995.

became partially flooded, which nearly broke Tony's heart – because of course the Mosquito's airframe was of timber construction. But all came to a happy ending when the T2 hangar was completed in 1996 and he was able to work on his beloved aeroplane in the dry. Tony called it *Spirit of Val* in memory of his wife who had backed the project to the hilt. Needless to say, Tony's Mosquito became one of the major attractions at YAM.

There was so much interest in what Tony was doing, it became fairly obvious to me that aircraft restoration projects taking place during visiting times were a great attraction. This view was shared by Bobby Sage as we had visited Duxford together several times and found that work in progress attracted a lot of attention. Although we at YAM were pleased indeed to accept modern jet aeroplanes such as the Lightning, Buccaneer, etc., from an interest point of view the fairly modern jet, whilst reflecting power and high performance, gave no impression of the complexities hidden behind the aluminium sheeting. Aeroplanes being worked on at

YAM, such as the World War One replicas being produced by the Rev. Norman Berryman and the Avro 504K which was the 'baby' of Maurice Voase, always drew a great deal of interest. It was my opinion that the museum would have developed more rapidly if we could have produced or housed aeroplanes capable of flying from the adjoining airfield. One only has to look through *FlyPast* magazine to see that the majority of air museums have such airworthy aeroplanes for the public to see.

Another acquisition was a Handley Page Herald, which we obtained from Jersey Airlines for the princely sum of one pound! The Herald was manufactured at Woodley, near Reading, and during one of Squadron Leader 'Hazel' Hazelden's visits to YAM we talked about the day when he took a Herald to Farnborough for the annual SBAC show and one of the Rolls-Royce Dart engines caught fire. Hazel 'put down' in a grass field, flying under some electricity cables and successfully ground to a halt. It was only because of his excellent ability and skill as a pilot that no-one was hurt. He was rightly awarded the Queen's commendation for his efforts. One of his colleagues, flying alongside him in a Hastings, asked him why he hadn't put out a 'May Day' call; typically he asked what bloody good that would have done!

Tony's Mosquito, Spirit of Val.

When my wife Mary visited the museum for the first time and saw the Herald, she told me of the occasion when the chairman of British European Airways, Sir Matthew Slattery, went to Woodley for a demonstration flight in the Herald. The company had hired an air hostess from Silver City for the day, and Sir Matthew and Lady Slattery were taken onto the airfield where this lovely, gleaming aeroplane stood. The sales director, Edward Manley Walker, introduced them to the pilot (again it was Hazel) and the crew. When he introduced the air hostess at the bottom of the steps, the very smart, attractive young lady stepped forward, held out her hand, and said: "Good morning, Sir Matthew....... and Lady Chatterley."

89

BRINGING THE BUILDINGS BACK TO LIFE

It was always our intention to reproduce on site an example of a briefing room, typical of those on each and every World War Two airfield. I was told of such a building which remained in a private garden of a property on the north side of the B1228 just past the entrance to the airfield. I obtained permission from the owner to visit what had been created in 1942, and Bobby Sage and I took a look inside. Bearing in mind that this was the very building in which he was briefed on 8th March 1943, prior to his fateful journey to attack the BMW engine factory in Stuttgart, it was indeed a very emotional moment for Bobby, as it was on his way back from the raid that he was shot down over Belgium.

The original building was not available to us, and so we erected a Nissen-style hut to act as a briefing room and lecture hall, and which would also act as an overflow facility for the NAAFI. We were fortunate in that some buildings (rather derelict, it has to be said) were being dismantled at nearby Acaster Malbis. One of these had been used as a military hospital during the war, and the owner very kindly offered it to us providing we would dismantle and remove it. Jack Kilvington and the team carried out the transfer to Elvington, and the pieces were rebuilt and sited between the existing NAAFI and the main exhibition hall. This turned out to be a rather costly undertaking, as we also included public toilets and storage facilities. It became known as the Elvington Room. As soon as this became available, the very hard-working and supportive Guy Jefferson reproduced a typical briefing room facility, which included a unique piece of film shot in black and white at Elvington in 1944 by the French squadrons. Derek Reed played a major part in getting this film. Once established, the general public were invited to view it at fixed times during the day and the whole project created an enormous amount of interest.

Watch tower at Elvington, March 1944.

77 Squadron memorial at Elvington.

Another significant development occurred when Bobby Sage and Dennis Sawden sought to reinstate the 77 Squadron Association, and their efforts were justly rewarded. Each subsequent year up to 2010 the squadron reunion was held at Elvington. Robert was appointed chairman of the association and with a small committee they raised funds for and designed the impressive 77 Squadron memorial which stands at the entrance to the museum. There were two characters that we called the 'Two Ronnies' – Ronnie Holmes and Ronnie Stewart – who also were very involved in this project. The association went on to commission a stained glass window which was placed in the Elvington village church and which is a fitting memorial not only to 77 Squadron but to many others.

With the establishment of 77 Squadron Association's link with Elvington and because of the publicity it generated, I was approached by the actor Derek Bond (who played a major role in *Scott of the Antarctic* to name just one production) whose brother Kenneth had served as a squadron leader pilot at Elvington but had gone missing on a raid on Laon, France, on 22nd April 1943. Derek and his mother requested the planting of a rose in memory of Kenneth and this was duly done in the rose garden, which is still lovingly tended by Walter Eland. It transpired that Group Captain Charles Hobgen (later to become chairman of 77 Squadron Association) had been the navigator in Kenneth Bond's crew. All the crew escaped the crash except Kenneth. Sadly, the flight engineer who escaped captivity and returned to England, was killed after the war ended in the only fatal accident involving Halifaxes at Clifton Moor, when he was in the crew flying in a Halifax for breaking up at the YARD at Water Lane. How sad that he'd escaped the enemy only to be killed in peace-time. A plaque in his memory is installed in the Roman Catholic Church on the Water Lane estate in York. I had witnessed this accident when I was on the airfield all those years ago.

By the mid 1990s we had constructed a lot of new buildings and had renovated and extended most of the original ones, and here I would like to pay tribute to Roy Handley and his company, based only a few hundred yards from the museum site. He played a massive part in the establishment of YAM. For example, digging out for the foundations for the T2 hangar

Elvington control tower after restoration in 1986.

Three major role players with the author, 2009. Bill Lord, author, Kath and Roy Handley.

The chapel.

involved the removal of hundreds of cubic feet of earth, which Roy was able to 'accommodate' on his land. Roy visited the museum almost daily, enjoying a cup of coffee in the NAAFI, regaling us with many amusing stories and bringing a light-hearted approach to everything. I can't tell you how often we phoned him with a cry for help, and the response was always the same – immediate and forthcoming.

Another major contribution from Roy, much later, was the construction of the chapel. The help he gave us in erecting this and many other buildings was invaluable. The main idea behind building the chapel was to provide a place of tranquillity where visitors could take a break and spend a few minutes thinking perhaps of loved ones they'd lost during the war. The foundation stone was laid in August 1995 by Air Vice-Marshal Harry Southgate, a long-time patron.

It was decided that the building should be in the style of a Nissen hut, in keeping with other buildings on the site. Once again, we had a lot of support for this venture – the wooden cross on the wall at the east end of the chapel was made by craftsmen at York Minster, and it was donated by the Dean and Chapter. Most of the internal fixtures and fittings came from the church at RAF Scampton near Lincoln. Silver flower vases were given by RAF Church Fenton and the beautiful kneelers were embroidered by members, wives of members and friends of the museum. The service of dedication was held in October 1996 and was conducted by the RAF's chaplain-in-chief, the Venerable P.R. Turner. And how fortunate we were that we had two padres at YAM, both ex-RAF, the Rev. Leonard Rivet and the Rev. Norman Berryman. Both had had distinguished careers in the Second World War, Leonard as a navigator with a squadron in North Africa and Norman carried out thirty-seven operations on Lancasters, as a flight engineer.

Derek Reed, in the early days of the museum, instigated a beautiful leather-bound book of remembrance, and over the years several hundred names have been added. These have been written in a most attractive script by Mandy Burgess, the calligraphist wife of Squadron Leader 'Budgie' Burgess.

Fitting the starboard outboard engine.

June 1996 assembly commences.

CHAPTER 6

Fundraising and Museum Life

With such rapid development on site, we realised that we must have stricter control over expenditure, and most Tuesday mornings I had informal meetings with members of staff and volunteers, including Jack Kilvington, Peter Slee, Ron Pontefract, and Peter Dowthwaite. Fortunately as most of the workers were volunteers, our expenditure on wages was minimal, and at no time did we intend to borrow or mortgage anything to raise cash. I suggested, and it was accepted by the team, that we should create a reserve emergency fund, and by 1998 this had built up to about £100,000. Obviously the lottery fund and the Canadian branch had made considerable contributions and local sponsors had helped with cash donations. We realised that whilst the capital asset value was increasing dramatically, revenue would have to be generated in order for all our buildings to be maintained, and because of their size the costs would be considerable and on-going. Furthermore, whilst we were acquiring and re-creating old aeroplanes, they too would have to be kept ship-shape in order to attract the public. It was obvious, like any business, we had to keep down overhead running costs if we were to survive.

One of our major successes in creating revenue was the introduction of corporate days and whilst a number of our volunteers were not too happy about the idea, we did raise considerable income from such companies as Ford Motors, Jaguar cars, and various other similar organisations. The income was mostly created by the museum hiring the airfield from the Ministry of Defence and sub-letting, benefitting too from things like NAAFI and shop sales. One event (although not involving the airfield) was when we were approached by Yorkshire Television who were contracted to produce a film in conjunction with an American company, concerning World War Two called *Till We Meet*. Obviously we were delighted to accommodate the film crew and it involved several American and British actors including Michael York. We had created a small shop in the NAAFI and I recall that Betty Harris did a roaring trade in small dolls dressed as aviators, complete with helmets and goggles. The film crew spent about two weeks on site during which time we had to close to the general public, but we were compensated by Yorkshire Television. It was fascinating to see how quickly film-makers can create temporary buildings which, on film, looked to be the real thing. There was a particularly friendly atmosphere on the site and YAM volunteers were a little sad when the project was completed. The film was shown in three episodes on ITV.

'Wall of bricks'.

Rather a lot of ideas for fund-raising were suggested, some of them impractical, but one which I did follow up in the early 1990s, was the suggestion that we should have a raffle with one large prize of a Morris Mini. I approached the main dealer in Leeds who incidentally supplied my company with staff cars, and he kindly agreed to supply the prize car at a substantial discount, since the money was being raised for charity. We produced tickets and distributed them amongst as many YAM members as possible and I think our target was about £5,000. Initially, the tickets sold well but by the time of the draw date we were struggling to cover the actual costs. Finally, the draw took place but the lady winner decided that she didn't want a Mini and she'd prefer the money instead. She had checked the list price which I think was in the region of £4,000. I then had the embarrassing job of explaining to her that our actual purchase price was something less. Fortunately for us, the lady understood and accepted the cash amount we'd paid. Our surplus turned out to be a disappointing hundred or two rather than the thousands of pounds we had anticipated – not one of our more profitable ideas.

I've already mentioned the brick fund under the supervision of the two Bettys, Hunt and Harris, but a major contribution for this fund came from Doug Sample in Canada who took up the cudgel with names and messages being relayed to YAM for eventual inclusion in the 'Wall of Bricks'. With this great help from the Canadian branch of the museum, by 1998 we had raised in excess of £40,000. Once the hangar was completed we recruited a competent and artistic bricklayer to build the decorative and none load-bearing wall.

Signed bricks.

Once we had completed the Handley Page hangar but before we'd put any part of the Halifax into it, I thought it rather a good idea to hold a band concert with music of the 1940s and 1950s. Jack Kilvington booked a local York dance band that specialised in Glenn Miller style music; and this event was a great success giving publicity to the museum and much needed money for our coffers.

One of the unsung heroines of YAM was a dear lady, Mrs. Ada Hillard. One day she was flown into the airfield and the young pilot introduced her as having an interest in World War Two aviation. It turned out that her family had owned a string of supermarkets in the Yorkshire area and on her very first visit and over a cup of coffee in the NAAFI, she offered me a cheque for any amount I could specify. I was somewhat embarrassed but suggested that £10,000 would be very acceptable. And so it was! We never did find out why she came to Elvington or what prompted her interest in aviation.

A husband and wife team who headed a well-known York family charitable trust visited the site frequently and were extremely supportive of our project. In one instance, they offered to pay for the re-surfacing of the wartime perimeter track and with the minimum of fuss they donated £20,000 for that particular work. They also gave us money for improvements to the NAAFI building, but they themselves always kept a very low profile. At the time, they asked that I did not publicise their names and to respect their wishes I will not do so now, but the museum will be eternally grateful for their generosity.

Further income was generated by the writing and publication of aviation books, and the late Sir Gus Walker, who became one of our most distinguished patrons was a fitting subject for one such. Upon his death, Lady Brenda Walker, with the help of Ian Wormald, placed many of his personal belongings including many photographs, into the YAM archives. It occurred to me at the time that no-one had written a biography of this remarkable man, a senior RAF officer, and I put the idea to Dennis Sawden – a retired squadron leader and one of the museum's tireless supporters – that if he was prepared to do the research the story would make fascinating reading. Dennis kindly agreed to take on the project with the approval of Lady Brenda and after many months of work YAM produced, with the help of Tom James, *Our Tribute to Air Chief Marshal Sir Augustus Walker*. The book raised in excess of £10,000 for the museum.

Air Chief Marshal Sir Augustus Walker GCB CBE DSO DFC, patron of YAM.

REUNIONS

Once the NAAFI had been extended we encouraged the ex-Halifax squadrons to hold their reunions at Elvington, and what a success they were. One such occasion which became established as an annual event was that of Halifax Coastal Command squadrons and the organiser, who became a close personal friend, was John Bell – a pilot awarded the Croix de Guerre for sinking German U-boats in and around the Bay of Biscay. About that time, I asked Mike Usherwood, a life member at YAM, if he would approach the Imperial War Museum with a view to obtaining any wartime films they may have had showing Halifaxes in service during the war.

Mike came back with a fascinating film showing a 58 Squadron Halifax carrying out a wheels-up landing at RAF St. Athan in South Wales. At the next Coastal Command reunion we ran this film to the assembled audience and to everyone's delight the crew involved were present. It transpired that the first member of the crew to emerge from the aeroplane was the pilot. Much raucous leg-pulling followed and many cries of: "What's all this about the pilot being the last out?" The Coastal Command squadrons were particularly relevant to the Yorkshire Air Museum, as the part of Friday the 13th we obtained from the Outer Hebrides was from one of their aeroplanes. One outcome of these reunions was that we located the pilot who, to our benefit, had carried out the belly-landing with Halifax HR792.

A truly remarkable story was told to me at one of the Coastal Command reunions. (And here perhaps I should explain that the squadrons who attended were those which had used the Halifax as their main tool, so in actual fact those present each year included the meteorological squadrons who, by the end of the war, were also based at Stornoway on the Outer Hebrides, along with 58 Squadron.) This particular evening I was sitting near John Bell and the subject of the emergency landing ground at Carnaby was raised. Carnaby, near Bridlington, had a huge runway – over 3,000 yards long and several hundred yards wide, with extensive grass under and over shoots at each end. It was opened in 1944 and by the end of the war over 1,000 emergency landings of all types of aeroplane had taken place there. This quite extraordinary story concerned a Halifax III from 58 Squadron, which had been on a sortie over Skagerrak, at night, attacking surface shipping. It carried a crew of eight including an additional wireless operator/air gunner to operate the extra radar which Coastal Command used. The skipper, who also attended the Elvington reunion, was Neil Lawson.

The aeroplane suffered an explosion underneath and to the rear of the fuselage, presumably an anti-aircraft shell. Obviously very alarmed, Neil instructed Frank Smith, the WOP/AG to investigate the damage and let him know what he found. After some time with no response from Frank, the skipper asked the flight engineer, Ken Magness, also to investigate the incident. Ken reported back on the intercom that a substantial part of the floor of the fuselage had disappeared, including the H2S scanner (i.e. the radar dome) and that there was absolutely no sign of Frank Smith. Due to the damage, the compass was inoperative and they were also getting low on fuel, so the crew asked for instructions and it was suggested that, as Stornoway was fog-bound, they should head for the emergency landing ground at Carnaby. At this stage in their flight they assumed that Frank had accidently fallen through the hole in the fuselage.

Neil made his approach to Carnaby with Ken Magness warning him that they were now desperately short of fuel. Carnaby ground control informed Neil as he came in to land that there was a body suspended beneath the rear fuselage, and the 'body' turned out to be the WOP/AG Frank Smith, who was unconscious. It transpired that Frank had fallen through what had been the scanner dome and his parachute harness had hooked onto the mechanism of the H2S scanner. As the aeroplane landed, Frank's intercom microphone situated on his oxygen mask had scraped the runway and remarkably prevented injury to him.

Needless to say I found this a riveting story and perhaps my face registered some doubt about its authenticity. John suggested that I should turn round in my chair and speak to a gentleman called Frank Smith who, with a very large grin on his face, confirmed that this tale was 100% true. Later in the evening I met Neil Lawson and he too assured me of its accuracy, adding that before he had finished taxiing on the Carnaby runway, all four engines had run out of petrol and stopped!

A sequel to this particular story occurred when in the mid 1990s I met a flying control officer whom I'd known during the war, who presented me with some paperwork compiled by air traffic controllers recording unusual incidents which had occurred during the war, and the first item I read detailed 58 Squadron's Halifax involved in the incident.

At a later Coastal Command reunion, John Bell told me another extraordinary story about two men in a boat, but as I couldn't remember the details I got in touch with John recently and asked him to fill me in. Here is John's own account of that very strange incident.

"I was nearing the end of my first tour of ops on Whitley aircraft with 502 Squadron at St. Eval when on May 19th 1942, I was sent in Whitley Z6734 on a training exercise with the submarine *Thunderbolt* off the south coast. On arrival at the rendezvous I was told to delay the exercise for thirty minutes. To waste time, I decided to fly due south for fifteen minutes into the Western approaches and then return to the rendezvous. After about fourteen minutes flying due south a small boat was spotted on the port bow, much to my amazement, so I went to investigate. In the boat were two men in army uniform waving oars and very excited. We notified group and were told to stay with the boat and await instructions.

"We spent the next four and a half hours circling the boat at low level so as not to attract enemy radar. A message from group was received saying that assistance was on its way to rescue the two men. Unfortunately, I was not able to witness the actual rescue as we had to return to base due to lack of fuel.

"It was not until 1962 or 3 that I heard the full story. An extract from the book *The Amateur Commandos* was published in a daily paper, and I contacted the paper who in turn contacted Mr. Cuthbertson (one of the commandos). He arranged to visit me and over a few beers told me all about the escapade. Two very bored men in the army dental section decided to have a go at the enemy themselves. They took a fishing boat with an outboard engine from a beach in Cornwall and armed only with revolvers set off for France. They arrived and had a 'recce' before being surprised by some German soldiers. They returned to their boat and set off back to the UK. Unfortunately for them they ran out of fuel about thirty miles off the English coast and had only two oars to propel the boat. Then out of the blue came my lumbering Whitley, a sight for sore eyes, just when they had given up hope. They were picked up by a Polish destroyer, which gave them a real shock as they thought it was German.

"They were taken back to the UK where they were court-martialled and sent to the glass house. Mr. Cuthbertson's friend went to New Zealand after the war but was sadly killed in a car crash, and Mr. Cuthbertson died in Newcastle about three years ago.

"How luck plays its part in our lives."

When John sent me this story, he very kindly included in his letter the comment: "With regard to our reunions at Elvington we all thoroughly enjoyed them, mainly because of the friendly way we were treated by you and your staff, so thanks again."

In 1944 I was on a course at Radlett on production test flying the new Halifax III and it was then that I first came across the famous Jim Mollison, husband of Amy Johnson, and Lettice Curtis, who were both members of the air transport auxiliary. Needless to say, I was more than a little surprised when Lettice and a flight engineer took off in one of the Halifaxes. They were collecting the new aeroplanes which we had test flown for delivery to the RAF. I then learned that Lettice had qualified to fly any of the four-engined 'heavies'.

When I was at the museum I felt it important that we should have some of these well-known aviation personalities associated with us and as Lettice had frequently flown in and out of the county collecting and delivering various types of aeroplane, I approached her and was delighted when she agreed to join us at Elvington. Along with Doug Sample we had some most enjoyable evenings in a local hostelry, when much reminiscing and a fair amount of imbibing took place. Considering her war-time efforts and achievements, it seems grossly unfair that she never received any official recognition – and this applies to most of her colleagues. Having had the privilege of looking through her log book and seeing just how many different types she flew, I feel that not many RAF pilots could have claimed similar experience. Lettice has written several books since the war including *The Forgotten Pilots* and her autobiography, and very well worth reading they are.

Each year we tried to base an open day on some special feature of World War Two aviation, and after considerable research I managed to locate a female special operations executive wireless operator who'd been parachuted into France. These special, very secret flights took place from Tempsford, near Sandy in Bedfordshire, where a squadron of Halifaxes specially equipped were used for flying agents into occupied countries, and also dropping supplies. So secret was each operation that the aircrews were not identified with the 'Joes' as they were called, i.e. no names were exchanged, and obviously

Lettice Curtis in the cockpit of a Halifax during the Second World War.

all these flights took place at night by moonlight at low level. After considerable digging, I managed to find the name of the pilot – Wing Commander Ratcliffe – who had flown a 'Joe' by the name of Yvonne Cormeau into France, and we were delighted when they both agreed to visit us on one of our open days. Dennis Sawden organised one of the RAF parachute teams to carry out a special drop in Yvonne's honour. This was a particularly joyous day when the pilot and his still unknown passenger were introduced for the first time. For this special occasion, the late John Rayson GAvA, produced a splendid oil painting of a Halifax carrying out a drop in France and John presented the painting to Yvonne, who was delighted to accept it.

Talking of John, he was one of our keenest supporters and one who did so much for the museum. He and his wife Barbara ran a shop in Harrogate which specialised in the sale of John's paintings. He and I were very close friends and when tragedy struck in the devastating form of motor neurone disease, the first affected parts of his body were his hands and arms. Because of his love of the museum I proposed that in the circumstances they may like to take over the running of the YAM shop. This they agreed to do and with Betty Harris's support the move took place.

John's health deteriorated rapidly, resulting in his death far too early at the age of sixty. Barbara then approached us with the idea of putting on a display of aviation and motor sport art. And in June 1995 we held the Wings and Wheels art exhibition. Because of John's association with the guild of aviation artists, she was able to contact many of the top UK talents who agreed to put on a display, with part of the profits going to the Motor Neurone Association.

David Shepherd, well known for his superb wildlife and aviation paintings, agreed to come as guest of honour. The event was a huge success, and after lunch in the NAAFI, David was asked to make a short speech. His talks can contain some rather colourful language and after lunch, one of the visiting ladies followed me out of the NAAFI and tapped me on the shoulder saying that she didn't think it was appropriate for a member of the Church to use language like that! She thought she'd been listening to the Bishop of Liverpool, also David Shepherd and a well-known cricketer. She was quite happy after I'd diplomatically put her right.

Tom James, a life member of the museum and owner of a printing company in York helped in the publication of my book *The Unbeaten Warrior Returns* to raise funds for the museum. Credit also should go to Dennis Sawden who edited the book and offered a lot of advice. It was Dennis and Tom again who produced a small guide book which was sold to visitors for £1 and raised a great deal of money. The booklet gave a summary of the history of the museum and a plan of the site, which included names which we'd given to various roads on the site commemorating local aviation worthies such as Barton Road, Cayley Road, Calmel Road and Gus Walker Road. Financially this guide book was a winner.

SUPPORT OF ALL SORTS

There were many members who not only contributed to the success and running of YAM, but also brought fascinating personalities to the site. One such was the late Bob Davies who flew Halifaxes with 578 Squadron at Burn, near Selby, and who in the post-war years played a major role in the squadron reunions which took place each year in York. Bob's hobby was the ownership of extremely large, powerful American cars – Buicks, Cadillacs, etc. Unannounced, he would arrive from London in one of these monsters and his first request was the same every time: could he drive his 5 litre vehicle at high speed up and down the runway? Another member with similar motorsport interests was Arnold Burton, who had also served in the RAF. A member of the famous Burton tailoring family, his peace-time hobby was owning and running high speed cars. Amongst his exotic cars was a British hand-built Noble, and on one occasion he was keen to see if this car could reach its claimed 160 mph. We obtained permission for him to carry out this exercise, but it was only when he arrived on site that I realised he intended that I should accompany him. Once we'd set off on the runway it was my job to call out the readings on the speedometer. Needless to say, the 160 target was reached, but with one very pale passenger.

I'd like to add that Arnold Burton was one of our most generous patrons.

Another hard-working member who stands out in my memory was the late dear old Malcolm Laycock, who had had to take early retirement because of disability. Malcolm brought onto the site his 'rescue' vehicle and consequently every time we needed something lifting Malcolm was called to the scene. He was usually the first on the site in the mornings and I think of him with affection and gratitude. His greeting was always the same, "'Ello Mr. Chairman". Malcolm seemed to typify the friendly atmosphere which had been created at the museum.

'Team Hooligan'. Author and Arnold Burton with the Noble car.

Another interesting character was Tony Pickard, an ex-submariner. After his career in the Royal Navy he had trained as a steel erector and when we came to construct the Handley Page building, his expertise was invaluable. As one would expect from someone who had spent many years under the sea, Tony was fearless. The trouble was, however, that his service life may have encouraged him into enjoying the odd tipple. My problem was to encourage the steel erection before lunch and to persuade him not to go up afterwards.

One of our keen and dedicated volunteers was the chairman of the 10 Squadron Association, the late Doug Dent, who had served with the unit which flew Halifaxes out of Melbourne, Yorkshire. Each year Doug would organise a reunion at Brize Norton, where 10 Squadron were flying VC 10s. Doug suggested that he might ask the commanding officer at Brize if on one of their training flights a VC 10 might be able to over-fly Elvington and this was arranged for one of our open days. The day duly arrived and the jet transport made a very low approach over the airfield with flaps and undercarriage down and all lights blazing. When it reached the museum site, the pilot put on full power and climbed steeply away. With several hundred cars parked at YAM and to much amusement and some annoyance the vibration set off quite a few alarms.

A memorable special event occurred when the late Doctor Mike Edwards, BAe director and YAM trustee organised one of the last Buccaneers to be flown into Elvington from Warton – this was S.2 XN974 and it flew in on 19th August 1991. This event attracted a huge number of visitors and what an impressive sight it was. The Buccaneer taxied to 'our' end of the airfield with its outer wings folded in its naval configuration.

Not too many aviation historians realise the affection the Buccaneer crews had for their aeroplane. As a result of the museum's acquisition, many former aircrew were to visit Elvington and ultimately were to form their own aircrew association of which I am proud to say I am an honorary member. Subsequently, the association purchased their own Buccaneer, S.2B XX901,

Buccaneer flown in to YAM, manufactured at nearby Brough.

which had been used in the Gulf War and which now resides at the Yorkshire Air Museum. The annual Yorkshire Air Spectacular eventually replaced these open days and attracted several thousand visitors.

I have already referred to the problem in the late 1980s, of raising income to progress as we all knew we could. By coincidence at that time I attended a model aeroplane show at Ripley Castle near Harrogate, and I was surprised and impressed by the size of the models and how well they were being flown by radio control. I introduced myself to the organisers and complimented them on the show and I met the man himself, David Tappin. Our meeting turned out to result in one of the most successful contributions I made at that time to the museum's finances. It occurred to me, having watched the show at the castle, how much better it could be if presented at the much bigger Elvington airfield, where we had all the facilities including public access (albeit with difficulty) and car parking space. As a result, I paid a visit to the commanding officer at Church Fenton, Group Captain Keith Walters, who also controlled flying at Elvington.

I put the idea to him of organising a model air show over a weekend, and he agreed that we could go ahead with the proviso that a proportion of the profits (if any) should go to the Royal Air Force Association. Consequently, I invited David over to the museum to have a chat, and he was delighted with the idea that he could make use of the airfield. Eventually, the show went from strength to strength and became an annual occurrence with a mixture of model flying and full-sized aeroplanes. The Yorkshire Air Spectacular became a well-known international event which also raised money for YAM. David was intrigued by what he saw at the museum and offered his services to help in any way. Well known for his likeable personality and his light-hearted attitude to most things, I suggested that he might consider becoming the museum's fundraiser. He readily agreed and we came to an understanding whereby he could retain a small percentage of any funds he raised, to cover his expenses, and this proved in the long term to be an excellent arrangement.

LECTURES

One idea which I'd had earlier was the possibility of arranging lectures on aviation matters which could take place in the evenings in the NAAFI building (later they were held in the Elvington Room). When I put this idea to David he was full of enthusiasm. Of all our ideas not simply to raise money but to publicise our existence at Elvington, this lecture programme organised by David must go down as one of our most successful ventures.

Lecture evening. L to R: Guy Jefferson, 'Bud' Morgan (US pilot of B17 Memphis Belle), and Derek Reed.

It may be of interest to list just a few of the better known speakers. One who springs to mind was the German general, Günther Rall, who 'downed' in excess of 300 Allied aeroplanes mainly on the eastern front, and who in the post-war years became the head of NATO Air Forces.

A YAM volunteer much involved with the programme was Guy Jefferson, and after this particular lecture he asked the general how he felt about shooting down so many Allied airmen and then coming over here to lecture to us? The general replied with a smile on his face, "Well, next time I'll join the Royal Air Force". The day after, I took the general along with David, on a tour of York, and he was intrigued to see in the Guildhall (which had been damaged by the Luftwaffe) an inscription referring to the so-called 'Baedeker' raid, and much to my surprise he was unaware that we referred to some of the raids as such. Karl Baedeker was a German travel writer and in the 1930s wrote several tour guides which included quite a number of UK cities, and several of those described in his guides were raided during the conflict. We entertained the general and several other guests to dinner at The Old Rectory at Sutton-on-Derwent. After finishing his main course, Günther left some roast potatoes and a Yorkshire pudding on his plate. "If you don't want that, Sir, could I finish it for you?" So said David, to the extreme embarrassment of yours truly.

Another most interesting character I spent some time with was the ex-Luftwaffe Colonel Hans-Joachim 'Hajo' Hermann who instigated the German night-fighter system referred to as 'The Wild Boar', in German *Wilde Sau*. He worked very closely with Galland and Goering.

A fascinating lecture was given by the famous Air Vice-Marshal 'Johnnie' Johnson. These talks were usually held on Friday evenings and with such well-known personalities attending I was always delegated the duty of meeting and greeting the speaker. In the case of Johnnie I stood outside the NAAFI building with several hundred members of the audience milling around. I approached the great man and extended my hand but no-one had warned me that sometimes his language could be somewhat rich, and his opening words were: "What silly bugger directed me to come here via Malton when I was coming from the south of England?" It goes without saying that the silly bugger was our friend David. I was so taken aback I didn't have the nerve to ask him why he didn't carry a map. Johnnie was indeed a rather fiery but very entertaining character and we had a thoroughly enjoyable evening, filling the Elvington Room and the NAAFI to capacity. As these lectures had become so popular and David was attracting such well known speakers, we found it difficult to accommodate all the visitors who wanted to come. So our friend Guy Jefferson stepped in again and did some of his electric wizardry, setting up a camera and television system whereby we could reproduce the lecture in the NAAFI building which is next door.

David himself was a keen follower of motorsport, and so we decided to try to attract some famous riders and drivers. One memorable evening was when John Surtees (the only person to win both Formula One and motorcycle racing championships) agreed to visit us. With an audience of several hundred people sat in the Elvington Room, and much to my consternation, John entered the room on one of the motorbikes and rode down the central aisle. This virtually brought the house down! Once again we were grateful for the absence of health and safety.

I think we had between 400 and 500 visitors for that particular lecture and it was past midnight before we could close the NAAFI.

I could not possibly list each and every lecturer, but some who are outstanding in my memory include Bill Bedford and Brian Trubshaw, both test pilots of renown. Also Robert Morgan, who flew the famous B-17 Memphis Belle, came over from the USA to deliver a most enjoyable lecture, a great coup for the Yorkshire Air Museum. Another American we entertained was Colonel Francis S. 'Gabby' Gabreski; he was the highest scoring P-47 Thunderbolt pilot in the US Army Air Force.

A motorsport man who drew a large audience was the famous Barry Sheen and these visits from such personalities which attracted such a large number of visitors, confirmed my view that a separate but adjacent motor museum would have added immensely to the success of YAM. But it was not to be.

Other notables who gave lectures included Dr. Gordon Mitchell, the son of R.J. Mitchell (designer of the Spitfire), and a character whom I found absolutely fascinating was the well-known Captain Eric 'Winkle' Brown CBE DSC AFC. Although a member of the Fleet Air Arm during World War Two and because he could speak fluent German, he became attached to the Royal Aircraft Establishment at Farnborough, Hampshire, where he test-flew every type of German aeroplane captured – for the purpose of comparison. In 1945 he went over to the continent and flew back to the UK just about every type of aeroplane that Germany had produced. He was a very humble and unassuming man with enormous experience of flying military aeroplanes.

One very happy event under the lecture programme was when we got together the German night-fighter pilot, Heinrik Rokker, and a member of one RAF crew he'd shot down, Eric Sanderson. We entertained them both socially (with wives) and presentations were made at Sherburn Aero Club. We were all entertained (plus David and Sylvia Tappin) by Ted and Shirley Kirkby who frequently acted as hosts by offering accommodation and hospitality at their beautiful home at Farnham, near Knaresborough. Ted had served in the RAF as a dentist and it was because of their hospitable invitations that some of our lecturers were able to come from afar to talk to us.

Another well-attended event was a lecture by an American designer, Lee Attwood, chief engineer with North American Aviation, who played a part in the production of one of the most successful fighter aeroplanes of World War Two – the P-51 Mustang. For an American to have flown the Atlantic to entertain us at Elvington was credit indeed to our organisation.

And yet another person we welcomed warmly for an evening's talk was Bill Reid VC. Bill had been awarded the decoration for flying his Lancaster, although severely wounded, to the target and returning and landing successfully back in the UK. A modest man, he gave Peter Slee and me the idea of creating a Victoria Cross room within the NAAFI building, showing drawings of all those airmen in Bomber Command who had been awarded this great honour.

I only wish I could quote the numbers of people who attended these lectures as the total must have been in the high thousands, but great credit should go to the YAM staff and

The Victoria Cross room.

volunteers who worked so hard to make these events so successful – Guy Jefferson in particular, who installed the communication system, and the NAAFI girls who catered for several hundred people before and after these events.

Apart from the RAF-diverted fly-overs, organised after a lot of string-pulling by Dennis Sawden and Ian Wormald, there was a very special occasion when Dick Chandler, a test pilot with BAe at Brough, flew in the only remaining Blackburn B2. This was a biplane designed and built in the 1930s as an ab initio trainer. The aeroplane which Dick flew in for us was the actual one recorded in Bobby Sage's log book when he flew it in the 1930s at Brough. The appointed day dawned and the weather was appalling with bad visibility and a low cloud ceiling. Nevertheless, in true Dick Chandler style he made it to Elvington. He then invited Robert to join him for a couple of circuits and naturally Robert, who seldom missed an opportunity to fly, accepted the invitation. Once in the air, the aeroplane was giving us a very nice display of aerobatics. Watching all this with me was Robert's wife, Peggy, and with a very nervous expression on her face she asked me if I thought Robert was at the controls. I assured her that I didn't think so, but I had my fingers firmly crossed behind my back.

On another similar day, Ian Wormald, who had by then left the RAF and was a test pilot at Brough, flew over and displayed the Pilatus which was the aeroplane then competing with the Tucano to replace the Jet Provost. Ian gave us a really magnificent aerobatic display and thrilled

B2 Blackburn, the only model left.

the crowds, which for these special days contributed considerably to the funds of the Yorkshire Air Museum.

CLOSURE OF RAF ELVINGTON

In 1992, some fifty years after the airfield had been opened, the Ministry of Defence decided to close RAF Elvington, and I organised with Group Captain Keith Walters, a commemorative closing-down ceremony on the museum site. Many of our patrons were present and our president, Wing Commander Robert Sage, in uniform, took the salute and a squadron of Jet Provosts flew past.

In recent years, the City of York councillors have opposed all applications to continue flying at Elvington and it seems that throughout the years York has been anti-aviation, even back to the twenties and thirties when the Airspeed company was established in Piccadilly, York. This same company was refused local flying facilities and had to take their first aeroplane – by road – to Sherburn-in-Elmet for its initial test flight. Those were the days when Nevil Shute Norway was involved with the company.

Following the closure in 1992, the Ministry of Defence decided to put the airfield on the market. This included the two-mile runway and some forty acres of concrete hard-standing, in all some 400 acres of land. The agents handling the sale on behalf of the ministry were a Leeds firm and the preparations for the outright sale took several years. Obviously, there was much speculation as to its future use, with local rumours abounding. The selling agents approached me and we came to an agreement whereby we, the museum, would hold the keys to the airfield and would act on their behalf to record and meet the potential buyers who visited us by prior arrangement. Not unnaturally, we at YAM were extremely concerned and hoped that whoever did buy the airfield would act favourably towards us. I found it interesting to meet the potential buyers and to hear their various schemes for the airfield's development, if they were successful. It would perhaps be unwise to mention the names of the interested parties, but some were of international renown.

Most importantly, our sponsor and neighbour, Roy Handley, discussed with us the possibility of his company A1 Haulage, putting in a bid for the airfield, and Roy told me that if successful he would give us – free of charge – some thirty acres of land adjacent to the museum site and which ran alongside the B1228 Elvington Road. It goes without saying that I and some of the other trustees were delighted at this proposition.

One scheme which I put forward at a trustees' meeting was to erect, with planning permission of course, more of the World War Two type buildings already on the museum site and create a motor museum, which would have been operated as a separate entity to YAM. I felt strongly that each would have attracted visitors to the other. We had close contact with the owner of a fleet of exotic and historic motor cars, and he was particularly keen on the idea as it would have enabled him to display his vehicles to the public and at the same time use the runway and hard standing for demonstration runs. Not all the trustees were in favour of this proposal; nevertheless, Roy insisted that we draw up an agreement detailing his offer before he submitted his tender. He insisted that I should sign the agreement on behalf of YAM. Apparently, the MoD in their invitation to those tendering suggested that the interests of the museum should be considered by the potential purchasers. Roy had plans prepared to accompany his tender, showing his proposed use of the airfield which indicated many and varied activities, but with control of sound emissions. Unfortunately, at the end of the day Roy's bid failed and another local tender was successful.

THE BARNES WALLIS TRUST

To return to the development of the museum, in 1992 I was approached by Bob Park, who was on the board of trustees of the Barnes Wallis Memorial Trust, and he told me that they were looking for a site in Yorkshire, not too far from the Howden area, to establish a display of the memorabilia and history of the famous Barnes Wallis. I have to admit that at that time whilst I was aware of the 'Dambuster' story, I was totally ignorant of the full and varied achievements of this remarkable man. Bob explained the strong link that Barnes had with Howden and in particular the construction of the R100 airship, built in an enormous hangar at Howden. Naturally after discussing this with my colleagues at YAM, we expressed the view that we'd be more than happy to accommodate the display, providing we could find a suitable building on site.

I was flattered when they invited me to become a trustee and whilst I attended some of their meetings I quickly realised that I had enough on my plate running YAM on a virtually full-time basis, and I therefore asked the late Betty Harris, our vice-chairman at YAM, if she would represent us on the Barnes Wallis Trust. After being made executive chairman of the museum in 1988, I had great pleasure in welcoming Betty as vice-chairman. Betty's husband Don had served in the RAF and she herself was a WAAF officer during the war, and she became one of YAM's most hard-working and loyal trustees. I could not have wished for a more supportive colleague and a dedicated worker who was sadly taken from us far too early in 1998. It was Betty who instigated the strong links with the education authorities in North Yorkshire, and it was she who played a major part in obtaining an example of the bouncing bomb which used to be on display at Elvington.

On site, we had the base of a war-time building and proposed to the Barnes Wallis Trust that it would be a suitable starting point to erect a structure to house their display. The trust contributed £2,000 towards the cost of completion, which was designed, with input from Tony Cockburn, to blend in with all the other buildings on site. In 1993, the display was officially opened by the son of Barnes Wallis and it became one of the major attractions at the museum. However, all the items remained under the jurisdiction of the Barnes Wallis Trust.

With the press and television present at the opening of the display, we were approached by a rather nervous German gentleman, who said, in very good English, that he hoped we would have no objection to him being with us on that day. He then went on to explain that he had been one of the anti-aircraft gunners on the Möhne Dam and that he would be so pleased to meet Barnes Wallis jnr., and the family. This naturally caused considerable interest, and at the official meal after the opening we placed him on the 'top table' next to Barnes. He left late in the evening with a very satisfied expression on his face and profuse thanks for our hospitality. Having been in contact with the Barnes Wallis family for many years, I applaud their purpose in educating the public not simply about the bouncing bomb, but about his many other remarkable achievements.

6 (RCAF) GROUP REUNION, JUNE 1990

We had so many visits from veterans who served with RAF 4 Group and RCAF 6 Group all based in Yorkshire, and it became apparent that they were considering the erection of memorials on the site to the many thousands who had served in World War Two. In the case of 6 Group, we planned one of the biggest reunions ever to take place at Elvington, which involved 800 Canadians who crossed 'The Pond' for this very special event. The team was led by General Reg Lane, who started his career flying Halifaxes at Linton-on-Ouse.

To cope with the expected guests, we had to hire one of the largest marquees in the north of England, where it was planned that Helen King and her NAAFI staff would provide a full three-course meal, to be followed in the evening by entertainment from the Royal Canadian Air Force band, which had also been flown over especially for the event. Prior to the reunion and after many months of hard work with the Canadian committee, marble memorial plaques had been produced, listing all the Canadian squadrons and their bases in Yorkshire. On the day of the unveiling, the veterans paraded on the site and I found this a most moving and memorable event. Not to be outdone, the veterans of 4 Group produced a similar marble plaque which was placed alongside their Canadian colleagues, all of which makes a marvellous background in the rose garden.

CHAPTER 7

The Roll-out

T2 HANGAR COMPLETED

By now, the T2 hangar was nearing completion and Friday, 13th September 1996 was getting nearer – our target date for the roll-out of the aeroplane. I mentioned earlier that I hadn't been too concerned about the fittings inside the fuselage, but strangely enough once we had been featured in *FlyPast* and *Aeroplane Monthly* magazines, offers from various parts of the UK and from France came flooding in. These included a complete tailwheel assembly which was from Halifax HX 271 and had been flown by 466 Squadron Royal Australian Air Force, shot down on a raid to Trappes on the 3rd June 1944. Some French civilians kindly offered it to us, and who flew it over? Japanese Airlines!

One of our original and very supportive friends at YAM was Squadron Leader Douglas Adamson, who had flown Halifaxes during the war. Douglas discovered a source of supply near

T2 hangar almost complete.

Friday the 13th assembled.

Duxford in Cambridgeshire where instruments were for sale, and he very kindly purchased a full set for the flight engineer's panels. Another sub-assembly which came to hand was the pilot's throttle box which included speed controls, airscrew controls, etc. These were very valuable gifts as they would have been extremely complex items to have had manufactured. In the meantime, our archives had been gradually filling up with more internal fittings: including wireless sets TR 1154 and 1155. Another piece of equipment gratefully received was the tubular metal frame which formed the pilot's escape hatch. In more recent years, John Hunt and Phil Kemp led a team which did a quite superb job inside the fuselage, and also produced a sound recording of engines starting-up. In addition, many of the pilot's controls were manufactured: flying control column, rudder bar, etc.

The T2 hangar measured 200 by 120 feet and slowly but steadily this piece of historical architecture rose from the ground. By early summer 1996, it was ready to take Friday the 13th as well as Tony Agar's Mosquito Spirit of Val. The purchase, assembly and construction of the T2 hangar ranked only with the Halifax rebuild itself in immensity, and its erection was a dramatic and impressive achievement for a small museum run by volunteers.

With our aeroplane nearing completion, I felt that we were in with a good chance of achieving our target roll-out date. We felt sure that a considerable number of people from both North America and France would like to be with us on that great day. Giving them as much notice as possible, the date was fixed and announced. The next problem was who should be invited to officiate? It was Ian Wormald who suggested that we should invite Sir Michael Knight

Satisfied YAM volunteers, June 1996.

to do the honours, and we were delighted when he accepted our invitation. Doug Sample in Canada organised the chief of the Canadian air force to attend, along with the Canadian ambassador in London. We had also planned that the Canadian ambassador would unveil a brick-built memorial naming the building the Canadian T2 Hangar. Groupes Lourds organised a lot of their members to join us, along with the French ambassador. Appropriately, the Earl and Countess of Halifax also accepted our invitation. Some of the surviving crews of the original Friday the 13th also accepted our invitation to join us, and local dignitaries including the Lord Mayor of York and the Lady Mayoress, were also in attendance. We estimated that on the day of the roll-out we could expect an audience (including members of the public) of about 3,000 people. In the event the figure was more than 5,000.

Some of the 'Thursday' volunteers.

My plans for the day included a full crew inside the Halifax, made up of Lettice Curtis representing the ATA, Fred Haynes, air gunner, and the rest of the crew made-up of pilots, navigators, wireless operators, etc. Also supposed to be included was the head of the

'Sunday and Tuesday' volunteers.

Canadian air force cutting the ribbon for the official opening of the hangar. But, as they say, the best laid plans... When it came to the actual event and someone handed him the scissors, one of my colleagues, a trustee no less, had failed to put the ribbon in the appropriate place – it was still sitting on my desk.

The big day dawned, bright and sunny, and to be perfectly honest I hadn't had much sleep the night before. The official proceedings were scheduled to begin at 11 o'clock, and as soon as we saw the general public arriving we realised that our estimate of numbers was going to be exceeded, by some considerable margin. It had been decided that I should be in the Elvington Room, which it was felt was the most appropriate place to meet and greet the VIPs. At about 10.45 a.m. I was called to the phone and informed by York City police that we had better get things moving as the queue of cars waiting to get in extended to the A64. Naturally, I had to leave my 'station' to find out exactly what was going on and I was confronted by the sight of our dear stewards nonchalantly chatting-up every driver and all the passengers in every

The author admiring the finished article.

car, before they entered the airfield where we had special permission to park. In my haste to persuade our volunteers to speed things up a bit, I came into contact with a barbed wire fence, doing myself a slight injury to a very sensitive part of my anatomy!

I have to confess that at this point I was becoming extremely worried. It was then brought to my attention that most of our important guests were held up in the traffic and our planned timing was obviously up the creek. The problem became even more apparent when YAM supporter Ken Cothliff arrived and told me that in order to get his VIP passenger there on time he'd driven more than three miles on the wrong side of the road. In the meantime, the museum's volunteers had arranged seating outside the T2 hangar, a guard of honour was present, the weather was superb; and approximately one hour late the official proceedings got under way.

I had persuaded a BBC radio announcer, Richard Clegg, to act as master of ceremonies, and he opened proceedings in a very professional manner to the assembled audience. Unbeknown to me and I suspect organised by Budgie Burgess, just about every type of aeroplane serving in NATO, was to over-fly the site, often in the middle of a speech. But what a show. From the Battle of Britain Memorial Flight to the French display team, and including RAF Tornados, a sentry AWAC, and too many others to mention, they put on a truly magnificent show for us. Perhaps in hindsight I failed to express my gratitude to those people behind the scenes who must have spent a lot of time, and pulled a lot of strings, in order to produce such a grand display.

Friday 13th September roll-out in front of some 5,000 visitors, 1996.

Several of our VIPs made speeches congratulating the museum on building the hangar and the Halifax. Sir Michael Knight made a truly interesting and humorous speech, paying great tribute to the Halifax's service during World War Two and pointing out that it had served in each and every RAF Command with the exception of Fighter Command. He said that it had proved to be an outstanding workhorse, but that not everyone was a fan, though most of those who had flown the Halifax did become very attached to her. Sir Michael quoted Max Hastings (admittedly no lover of Bomber Command, or indeed of the Royal Air Force) dismissing the Halifax as: "A workhorse of no breeding and alarming vices." However Sir Michael went on to say, "there's an old saying in this part of the world, 'there's nowt so queer as folk', and in any case, Mr. Hastings was wholly unqualified to comment". He concluded his speech by saying: "So no more chat. I don't get to give many direct orders these days, but here's one that gives me the greatest of pleasure – roll out Friday the 13th." With that, the hangar doors opened and led by flag-bearers and to a fanfare of trumpets, Jack Kilvington on our David Brown tractor did the honours. My plans for each of the crew to be announced as they stepped out of the aeroplane went by the board as hundreds of well-wishers disregarded all the barriers and rushed forward for a better view.

Lettice Curtis, Sir Michael Knight, and the author, 13th September 1996.

A truly magnificent day. Guests were invited to take lunch in the hangar, which had been beautifully laid out by the NAAFI staff, and I can remember Sir Michael saying that in all his experience in the RAF he'd never seen such an attractive layout which catered for several thousand people. How very sad I was that Robert Sage wasn't with us to witness the roll-out – I know it would have given him enormous pleasure and a justly appropriate amount of pride.

We had planned a 1940s style ball for the following evening, requesting that visitors should wear some appropriate dress. As we expected many turned up in their wartime uniforms, some of which seemed to have shrunk over the years, and I thought I could detect a distinct smell of moth-balls. Some of the sights will stay with me forever, especially the one of a respected RAF officer Ian Wormald and his wife, both dressed as 'Mrs. Mop', a character from the Tommy Handley wartime radio series 'It's That Man Again', complete with headscarves and curlers, pinnies, wrinkled stockings, and mops and buckets! At considerable expense, we'd booked a twenty-piece London band, led by Chris Smith – an outfit recommended by Doug Dent who had engaged this orchestra for several 10 Squadron events. And what a good choice. The evening went very well indeed and many of our Canadian friends had stayed over and joined in the fun. The Halifax had been rolled back into the hangar and was floodlit, with the band placed underneath the nose. The music was played in the Glenn Miller style and the whole evening was a huge success.

OTHER HALIFAX PROJECTS

During the 1970s the RAF had successfully recovered a Halifax which had been shot down and rested in a lake in Norway. This was Halifax II W1048 'S-for-Sugar' of 35 Squadron. It had force-landed in Lake Hokingen on 27th April 1942. Once recovered, it had been transported to the RAF Museum at Hendon, and an appeal for money to restore it was launched by the late Warrant Officer Paddy Porter. He put in a tremendous amount of work to persuade people to support the venture and some donations, including one from myself, were presented to Hendon. But to everyone's amazement we were informed that the RAF Museum had no intention of restoring the aeroplane and that it was their idea to exhibit it 'as recovered' from the lake. Again, all we Halifax enthusiasts were flummoxed, as to the best of our knowledge it would be the only whole aeroplane on display in an unrestored condition. Because of our success at Elvington, it made me feel extremely proud of what we, mainly volunteers, had achieved.

One of our early supporters was a young Canadian airline pilot, Karl Kjarsgaard. He visited Elvington many times and worked closely with Doug Sample. Although keen to help us, he was very anxious to find another Halifax for restoration in Trenton, Ontario. I think mainly because of the strong feelings held by Canadians who flew the Halifax and who wished to have one of their own. Another keen supporter of the Canadian Halifax restoration project was an ex-Halifax pilot Jeff Jeffrey DFC, and together they formed the Halifax Aircraft Association. They were subsequently successful in locating another Halifax NA337, a Mk VII, built by Rootes Securities at Speke, Liverpool. It had been hit by flak on an SOE mission with 644 Squadron and had crash-landed in Lake Mjosa, Norway, on 24th April 1945. With a great deal of effort they raised funds to have the Halifax recovered and dismantled ready for transportation to Canada.

I entertained the engineers from Norway who were planning to salvage the aeroplane and advised them on the correct lifting points, weights, etc. They did a superb job and the Halifax in its dismantled form was air-lifted in C 130 Hercules to Canada. A restoration team was formed and the whole project seemed to be financed without any problems, a very different picture from our Elvington Halifax. I offered our help and supplied them with the pattern for manufacturing the undercarriage legs and the front fuselage Perspex frame, plus drawings where necessary. Their restoration has been a huge success, but nowhere do we read of any credit to the Yorkshire Air Museum.

CHAPTER 8 Reflections

Since January 1999 and as I had hoped, much work on Friday the 13th has now been completed and many of the internal fittings are in position. Of some concern to me is the fact that, because much of the airframe is some sixty years old, a lot of time and effort will have to be spent on care and maintenance.

When I first thought of a Halifax reconstruction in 1983, frankly I really didn't know if it would eventually result in the making of a complete aeroplane. I found it hard to believe that over 6,000 were made and not one had been retained for a museum. The examples at Hendon and in Canada had to be recovered from watery graves. This fact was all the more ironic, and hurtful to me, when the squadrons flew their Halifaxes into the YARD at Clifton Moor. Some of these aeroplanes were brand new and whilst I cannot be too precise about the numbers, I think about 400 were scrapped.

YAM staff, Halifax workers and wives pose in front of Friday 13th 'the second', June 23rd 1996.

'Friday' starboard side in French colours.

My mentor throughout the project was my dear friend, the late Wing Commander Bobby Sage OBE AFC. I sometimes doubt whether, without his help, guidance, advice and encouragement, I would have persevered with the idea. I found it very difficult to understand the 'purists' who were anxious to criticise by making comments such as: "In the whole, it isn't a genuine Halifax." I know that through lack of genuine parts, we sometimes had to compromise – for example, the propeller pitch is incorrect but we had no choice but to work from the one and only blade we had available.

However, it is interesting to note that the criticisms didn't originate from any of the veterans, in fact the very opposite. Without exception, they were full of admiration for what we had achieved. There is no doubt that the existence of Friday the 13th at Elvington has become the chief attraction, and it is with considerable pleasure and some pride that I now read or see on television reference to the Halifax, which of course had always previously been over-shadowed by its brother-in-arms, the Lancaster. My only hope for the future is that it will continue to be maintained in its majestic form.

It is a great shame that I didn't keep a diary and an equally great shame that I did not record each and every person who helped me along the way, including those who made substantial donations and those who gave so freely of their time and effort. There was so much support, enthusiasm and goodwill from hundreds of people. A lot of them had, like myself, some connection with aviation during the Second World War, but had moved on to create new careers and interests in the subsequent thirty-eight years, giving little thought to their wartime activities. Could it be that some of them took the opportunity to rekindle their wartime friendships and the patriotism that existed in those dark days?

I find it difficult to believe that any one of the twenty or so of us in on the 'ground floor' of the Yorkshire Air Museum and Allied Air Forces Memorial could have imagined the growth and the support we were to receive. I think in all honesty Rachel Semlyen would admit that never in her wildest dreams could she have envisaged what was to develop from her original idea.

The extreme goodwill and enthusiasm which seemed to home-in in those early days is difficult to express in words – help from all corners of the UK as well as from Canada, USA, France, Germany and many other countries. And talking of France, one

Author presented with MBE by Sir Marcus Worsley, 1998.

126

achievement which went unnoticed for some reason was that when the Halifax project was nearing completion, our French friends were very enthusiastic and submitted the project for an award from their equivalent of our Royal Aeronautical Society. Our Halifax came second, and the prize was a very, very expensive, exclusive wrist-watch which was sent to Elvington. Earlier in this book I referred to the generosity of the French in providing our four Hercules engines and the tailwheel assembly for Friday the 13th and it is perhaps appropriate that the starboard side of the aeroplane has now been painted in French squadron markings.

Another gratifying event occurred in May 1998 when I received a letter from 10 Downing Street, and I was absolutely astounded to read that I had been awarded the Most Excellent Order of the British Empire. My first reaction was that someone was pulling my leg, especially as the letter was not very well typed on a very old-fashioned typewriter. The letter made it quite clear that I should not discuss this award with anyone until the official Birthday Honours List was published in June. It was only when the local press contacted me that I had to believe it! And to this day, I have never been sure who put my name forward. As I felt it was an honour for the museum as a whole, I decided not to go to Buckingham Palace to receive the award and instead the Queen's representative for North Yorkshire, Sir Marcus Worsley, Lord Lieutenant, came to Elvington with Lady Worsley to carry out the ceremony. This was in October 1998 and what an enjoyable day it was.

CONCLUSION

How does one summarise those sixteen years from 1983 to 1999? Regrets? Yes, I have a few. But the gratification and the pride continue. It is interesting to note that as I write there is some discussion regarding a Bomber Command memorial and where it should be sited. The Lincolnshire supporters are keen that it should be in their county and no doubt similar feelings will be expressed in East Anglia and in Yorkshire, but it would seem to me that the proper place would be in the City of London or at the National Arboretum in Staffordshire. Wherever they put it, one thing is for sure – there should be a memorial. I find it difficult to understand the post-war attitude to Bomber Command and surely whatever the rights and wrongs of the bombing offensive during the Second World War, we should all remember that those who served in whatever capacity were doing what they had been instructed to do – fighting for their King and country.

So many people keep in touch and only the other day a friend sent me a print-out of something posted on the internet. It was a report of a visit to YAM by the Cambridge branch of the Royal Aeronautical Society, which concluded: "The highlight of the visit was undoubtedly the conducted tour of the inside of the Halifax bomber, not normally open to the public, and arguably one of the best restoration projects that the UK's volunteer aircraft preservation movement has produced." And I'm told by many friends that it is frequently referred to as YAM's 'Jewel in the Crown'. Our original intention in forming the Yorkshire Air Museum and Allied Air Forces Memorial was to establish a fitting reminder of the sacrifice made by over 55,000 of Bomber Command who gave their lives and of whom many historians have been critical. I'm sure that the hundreds who helped in the creation of the museum feel as I do that we achieved our objective and more.

As to Halifax Friday the 13th, what can I say? Is it a restoration? A rebuild? A new-build? A recreation? Call it what you will. It is a tribute to so many people and it is my pride and joy.

A Tribute to the Author

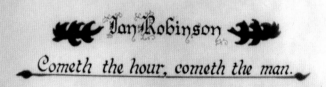

Home is the Halifax

The Handley Page Halifax was one of the most versatile and durable aircraft of its kind. It was also much maligned, although not by those who flew in it. More than 6,000 were built in twenty variant forms and there were few corners of the globe that did not at some time resound to the roar of its mighty engines.

In the hands of its aircrew it pressed home the tasks demanded of it and when torn by shot and shell or battered by the elements its construction was such as to permit it to struggle back to base, duty well done.

It seems strange that that which the enemy so signally failed to do we, as a nation, achieved with clinical, if thoughtless, precision. Once the war was over not one example of this worthy veteran was retained, to be honoured and revered in decent retirement.

Happily there are, however, men of vision. One of them, himself an erstwhile flight engineer with the Handley Page Company, who as a young man had helped test fly so many of the Halifax aircraft destined for fighting quadrons, was determined this deficiency in our aeronautical and Royal Air Force history should be remedied.

Together with a band of dedicated helpers and enthusiasts he set about recreating that which had been destroyed.

From nook and cranny, from stockpiles and storerooms, from far and wide, the often abused fragments of past giants were reclaimed to be given back their dignity and refurbished into that which they formed half a century ago. Phoenix like, a Halifax aircraft, Friday The 13th has risen from the ashes of disregard and contempt.

No matter that the roar of its mighty engines will not be heard over the Ridings of Yorkshire. No matter that its menacing black shadow will never glide across the green swards and silver waters of the Dales. The Halifax, proud warrior aircraft, has returned home to rest in Yorkshire. In the shadow of the Minster. At Elvington.

Every aviator who ever had the honour to crew or maintain the mighty Halifax, in particular those of us who served with 77 Squadron, owes a debt of gratitude to that man of vision.

Ian Robinson

Cometh the hour, cometh the man.

Home is the Halifax

The Handley Page Halifax was one of the most versatile and durable aircraft of its kind. It was also much maligned, although not by those who flew in it. More than 6,000 were built in twenty variant forms and there were few corners of the globe that did not at some time resound to the roar of its mighty engines.

In the hands of its aircrews it pressed home the tasks demanded of it and when torn by shot and shell or battered by the elements its construction was such as to permit it to struggle back to base, duty well done.

It seems strange that that which the enemy so originally failed to do we, as a nation, achieved with clinical, if thoughtless, precision. Once the war was over not one example of this worthy veteran was retained, to be honoured and revered in decent retirement.

Happily there are, however, men of vision. One of them, himself erstwhile flight engineer with the Handley Page Company, who as a young man has helped test fly so many of the Halifax aircraft destined for fighting squadrons, was determined this deficiency in our aeronautical and Royal Air Force history should be remedied.

Together with a band of dedicated helpers and enthusiasts he set about recreating that which had been destroyed.

From nook and cranny, from stockpiles and storerooms, from far and wide, the often abused fragments of past giants were retained to be given back their dignity and refurbished into that which they formed half a century ago. Phoenix like, a Halifax aircraft, 'Friday the 13th', has risen from the ashes of disregard and contempt.

No matter that the roar of its mighty engines will not be heard over the Ridings of Yorkshire. No matter that its menacing black shadow will never glide across the green swards and silver waters of the Dales. The Halifax, proud warrior aircraft, has returned home to rest in Yorkshire. In the shadow of the Minster, at Elvington.

Every aviator who ever had the honour to crew or maintain the mighty Halifax, in particular those of us who served with 77 Squadron owes a debt of gratitude to that man of vision.

Ian Robinson
Cometh the hour, cometh the man.

Presented by Group Captain Charles Hobgen, Chairman of 77 Squadron Association, to the author on September 14th 1996.

APPENDIX 1 — Wing Commander Robert Sage

Wing Commander Robert Sage's own account of his crash

On March 9th 1943 seven Halifax bombers of 77 Squadron were detailed as part of a force of 164 aircraft to attack the diesel engine works in Munich. Their role was to form part of the flare force, starting flares following the positioning of target illuminations, to give an aiming point for the main bomber force. The main armament consisted of nine containers of small incendiary bombs with one 1,000 lb high explosive bomb. Because of the long distance to be flown the aircraft carried two extra fuel tanks in the bomb bay.

I was the flight commander of B Flight and was at the time responsible for running the squadron pending the appointment of a successor to the previous commander, lost on operations. My normal aircraft was 'M' but this was under repair because of flak damage in a previous operation. 'J' was allocated in its place. My crew consisted of F/Lt Brian Barker (navigator), F/Lt Danny Bateman (signals), F/O Jack Adams (rear gunner), Sgt Johnny Walker (engineer), Sgt John Morris (mid-upper gunner), and Sgt Norman Crabtree (bomb aimer).

'J' took off from Elvington at 20.00 hrs in fair weather, followed at short intervals by the other six aircraft. Course was set for an assembly point on the Thames estuary, climbing to a pre-arranged altitude of 17,000 feet and speed adjusted to give an arrival time pre-arranged in order to concentrate the force.

Aircraft systems were tested during this period, and, in addition to some minor faults, the gyro master compass was found to be unreliable, so the pilot's magnetic compass had to be relied on for navigation. Crossing the English coast, some shocks were felt which it was thought might have been from friendly AA fire (not unknown), but there was no apparent damage and the flight continued uneventfully until, approaching the target area, the engineer reported serious loss of coolant from the starboard outer engine. It had to be shut down immediately and power increased on the other engines to maintain height.

The target could be seen, although not fully illuminated and the weapon load was released, before setting course for the return journey. Accurate navigation was difficult, not only was the gyro-compass out of action, but shutting down the starboard engine meant the loss of the only a/c generator which powered the navigation equipment. The fact that we had strayed off course was brought home when we flew over a large city, not on our planned route (thought to be Stuttgart) and we were subjected to the full and individual attention of the searchlights and AA fire. The aircraft may have been further damaged and some height was lost during the violent evasive manoeuvring which also introduced further uncertainties. We decided during a quiet period (about 2.00 a.m. on the following morning) that the importance of fixing our position justified unfeathering the shut-down engine so that the windmilling effect would run the generator and give power for at least a 'Gee' fix.

Whilst I was doing this there was a shattering burst of heavy cannon fire from behind and below causing heavy damage, including knocking out the two left-hand

Wing Commander R.J. Sage OBE AFC at Elvington.

engines and setting fire to the port wing. Mercifully the crew members were uninjured but clearly the aircraft was lost, so I gave instructions to abandon. When the crew had left, I abandoned the controls and made a dive for the lower escape hatch. I regained consciousness about half an hour later, lying across a railway line with my parachute in the telegraph wires through which I had fallen, causing facial injuries. I hid my parachute in a railway wagon standing in a siding, and with some difficulty because of a broken ankle, I made my way along the line to a workman's hut where I was shortly joined by a labourer who offered me food and went off to find help to get me away. He came back with the Gestapo. Unfortunately, he turned out to be a conscripted Polish miner who hoped to obtain concessions from them. His action was ill-advised because the French underground soon discovered what he had done and put him to death. It transpired that I had landed on the outskirts of Mons, not far from where my aircraft had crashed and was burning.

The other members of my crew had mixed fortunes. Very sadly, Jack Adams' body was found near his partly-opened parachute. All the others evaded immediate capture.

Brian Barker and Norman Crabtree were returned to this country by different routes within a few months. Danny Bateman, whose parachute had been damaged by cannon fire, remained free in an injured state for a few days, before being arrested by French police and becoming a POW like myself. Danny Morris evaded capture for about eighteen months before being apprehended by the authorities in Bordeaux. I have had no contact with Johnny Walker and do not know his story, except that I believe he evaded capture and returned to this country. A copy of the report made by Brian Barker on his return in 1943 is detailed in appendix two. Throughout his life he kept in touch with regular visits to the French family who had sheltered him. He enjoyed a long and successful career in the Yorkshire brewing industry, becoming managing director of Hull Breweries before his death.

Of the other six aircraft, five returned safely and one disappeared with its crew without trace. Altogether, eight aircraft were lost from the total force.

I think I can say this wasn't my day.

Most Secret Report K.16

OPERATIONAL RESEARCH SECTION (B.C)

REPORT NO. K.16

COPY NO. 1

Report of Loss of Aircraft on Operations

Aircraft: Halifax II (Z type) DT.734.　　　"J" of 77 Squadron.

Date of Loss: March 9/10th. 1943.　　　Target: Munich

Cause of Loss: Flak after engine failure.

Information from: F/Lt. B.D. Barker, Navigator.

Previous experience of informant:　　　5 operations in a Whitley. 3 in Halifax, and 18 sorties for Coastal Command. Shot down on second operation after returning to Bomber Command.

Remainder of Crew:

Pilot.	S/L. Sage	Fate unknown.
A/B.	Sgt. Crabtree	"
W/Op. A/G.	P/O Bateman	"
F/E.	Sgt. B.J. Walker	Escaped
M/U/G.	Sgt. Morris	Fate unknown.
R/G.	P/O K.A. Adam	"

Narrative

1. The aircraft took off from Elvington and flew a straight course down country to cross the coast at Dungeness. While crossing the Thames estuary at 9,000 feet a bump was felt and the crew suspected, although only half-seriously, that they had been fired at by A.A. guns. (There is no record of our guns firing in this area on this night.)

2. The enemy coast was crossed at about 15,000 feet with the aircraft still climbing. Gee was u/s, but the aircraft kept well on course and picked up the P.F.F. markers on the turning point. The aircraft then began to approach the target at 17,000 feet when the starboard engine failed. This failure followed loss of coolant from a leak whose origin is uncertain. (At the time, it was thought possible that the aircraft had been hit during the incident mentioned in para 1, but since there was no gunfire, the leak probably resulted from a mechanical failure.)

3. The aircraft was then approaching the target. P.F.F. markers were not seen but a quick run in was made and the bombs released.

4. The pilot set course along the briefed homeward route. He was able to maintain a height of 15,000 feet and to fly the aircraft in 3 engines without great difficulty.

5. Some difficulty was experienced in keeping on track and over Belgium the aircraft was flown straight and level in order that an astro-fix might be obtained. After a few minutes of straight flying at about 140 IAS. at 15,000 feet the aircraft suddenly received two heavy bumps at an interval of a few seconds. No enemy activity was seen beforehand and none followed immediately but it was presumed that the bumps resulted from two bursts of heavy flak.

6. Many fragments came through the aircraft from the first burst, one passing in through the floor between the navigator and wireless operator to damage the latter's panel. Immediately after the second burst, the port outer engine was reported to be on fire.

7. The crew was ordered to bale out and F/Lt. Baker (sic) was able to leave and land without difficulty. He saw nothing of the rest of the crew or of the final fate of the aircraft. He landed near Mons between 0200 and 0230 on March 10th.

8. Soon after he left the aircraft F/Lt. Baker (sic) saw flares fired up from the ground. These illuminated him to a disturbing degree and he felt that both then and when on the ground that his white parachute was unnecessarily conspicuous and that it would be better to have a dark parachute.

Comment

9. On this night, a change of wind caused all navigators some difficulties. It was unfortunate chance that carried this aircraft across a defended area while its position was being checked and so frustrated the crew's good attempt to fly it home from Munich in a damaged condition.

14743/3.
BC/S. 30270/ORS.
24th. July, 1943.

MOST SECRET

OPERATIONAL RESEARCH SECTION (B.C.)

REPORT NO. K. 16

COPY NO. 1

Report of Loss of Aircraft on Operations

Aircraft: Halifax II (Z type) DT.734. "J" of 77 Squadron.

Date of Loss: March 9/10th. 1943. **Target:** Munich.

Cause of Loss: Flak after engine failure.

Information from: F/Lt. B.D. Barker, Navigator.

Previous experience of informant: 5 operations in Whitley. 3 in Halifax, and 18 sorties for Coastal Command. Shot down on second operation after returning to Bomber Command.

Remainder of Crew:

Pilot.	S/L. Sage	Fate unknown.
A/B.	Sgt. Crabtree	"
W/Op. A/G.	P/O. Bateman	"
F/E.	Sgt. B.J. Walker	Escaped
M/U/G.	Sgt. Morris	Fate unknown.
R/G.	P/O. K.A. Adam	"

Narrative

1. The aircraft took off from Elvington and flew a straight course down country to cross the coast at Dungeness. While crossing the Thames estuary at 9,000 feet a bump was felt and the crew suspected, although only half-seriously that they had been fired at by A.A. guns. (There is no record of our guns firing in this area on this night.)

2. The enemy coast was crossed at about 15,000 feet with the aircraft still climbing. Gee was u/s, but the aircraft kept well on course and picked up the P.F.F. markers on the turning point. The aircraft then began to approach the target at 17,000 feet when the starboard outer engine failed. This failure followed loss of coolant from a leak whose origin is uncertain. (At the time, it was thought possible that the aircraft had been hit during the incident mentioned in para 1, but since there was no gunfire, the leak was probably resulted from a mechanical failure.)

3. The aircraft was then approaching the target. P.F.F. markers were not seen, but a quick run in was made and the bombs released.

4. The pilot set course along the briefed homeward route. He was able to maintain a height of 15.00 feet and to fly the aircraft in 3 engines without great difficulty.

5. Some difficulty was experienced in keeping on track and over Belgium the aircraft was flown straight and level in order that an astro-fix might be obtained. After a few minutes of straight flying at about 140 I.A.S. at 15000 feet the aircraft suddenly received two heavy bumps at an interval of a few seconds. No enemy activity was seen beforehand and none followed immediately but it was presumed that the bumps resulted from two bursts of heavy flak.

6. Many fragments came through the aircraft from the first burst, one passing in through the floor between navigator and wireless operator to damage the latter's panel. Immediately after the second burst, the port outer engine was reported to be on fire.

7. The crew was ordered to bale out and F/Lt. Baker was able to leave and land without difficulty. He saw nothing of the rest of the crew or of the final fate of the aircraft. He landed near Mons between 0200 and 0230 on March 10th.

8. Soon after he left the aircraft F/Lt. Baker saw flares fired up from the ground. These illuminated him to a disturbing degree and he felt that both then and when on the ground that his white parachute was unnecessarily conspicuous and that it would be better to have a dark coloured parachute.

Comment

9. On this night, a change of wind caused all navigators some difficulties. It was an unfortunate chance that carried this aircraft across a defended area while its position was being checked and so frustrated the crews good attempt to fly it home from Munich in a damaged condition.

14743/3.
BC/S. 30270/ORS.
24th. July. 1943.

ODE TO
THE HALIFAX

ODE TO THE HALIFAX

From the ashes of time the Phoenix has risen,
A World War 2 Halifax - Oh, what a vision.
She stands in her hanger for everyone to see
This plane which helped us all to be free.

This giant so gentle and easy to fly
In all kinds of weather she conquered the sky.
The crews had great faith in the way she performed
Her strength and her sleekness so perfectly formed.

BOMBER COMMAND

Memories of the Halifax imprinted on our brian -
The gunners in their turrets staring through the rain
Looking for the fighters somewhere in the gloom,
Their Brownings at the ready to send them to their doom

Flak all around the aircraft - the pilot steers his course
The Halle battles through it - a super fighting force.
"Left, Left" comes o'er the intercom, they're on the bombing run
The crew, all tense, wait til the deed is done.

"Bombs Gone" sounds on the intercom, now they're going down,
Then Bang and Flash, she's on her back and dropping like a stone.
An engine gone, damaged wing and heading for the ground,
But true to form she straightened out and soon was homeward bound.

Like a wounded stag she battled on - a fight against the odds,
Three mighty Merlins roaring loud - a challenge to the gods.
Then straight ahead a familiar sight - she'd made the base at last
That scarred and damaged Halifax, her toughness unsurpassed.

COASTAL COMMAND

Memories of this aircraft, the special coastal type
With extra tanks and radar and painted all in white.
She flies for hours and hours ranging the ocean wide
Searching for the U Boats with radar as her guide.

A contact on the radar and she prepares for an attack
With fuses set she battles through the U Boat's heavy flak.
The stick explodes and spray erupts all round that shiny nose
It couldn't survive the mortal blows and slowly down she goes.

In nineteen forty four to the Skaggerak she was bound
To sink the ships from Norway wherever they were found.
The bombs replaced the charges and she only few by night
With flares to light the ships below then bomb them by their light.

Flak hit a plane of fifty eight and one of the crew went missing
A hole gaped in the fuselage floor through which the wind was whistling.
Neil turned for home with a saddened crew to land on a 'Fido' runway
To find Frank hanging by his harness straps from the hole by the aircraft's doorway

THE MET. FLIGHTS

This long range plane with its extra crew
Was used to predict what the weather would do
Low over the sea she collected the gen
Then high in the sky she took readings again.

Whatever the weather they took to the sky
In daylight or darkness ready to fly.
Their task was essential for fighting the war
For bombing, for raiding and reasons galore.

SPECIAL OPERATIONS

The versatile Halifax on the hardstanding waits
Loaded and ready for the task that awaits.
Flying low over France to drop her supplies
To the fighting Resistance - our gallant allies.

She was there flying low on her clandestine ops
Taking S.O.E. agents to pre-determined spots.
When light signals indicated that all was clear
They parachuted down showing no signs of fear.

GLIDER TOWING

The Halifax like the Hurricane was used in many ways
And comments on her different roles were always full of praise
Beside her other duties the gliders she would tow
To help the Allied landings in the fight against the foe.

THE YORKSHIRE AIR MUSEUM

To all those brave crews who gave of their lives
'Friday the Thirteenth' means their memory survives
And we who are left with heads in the skies
Pay tribute to all who made Phoenix arise.

Tinko Bell (1997)

Index

INDEX